Analyzing Criminal Behavior

Gregory M. Cooper & Michael R. King

International Standard Book Number: 0-615-11937-9

IQ Design Publishing / Ogden, Utah

Institute of Investigative Science
www.IOIS.net

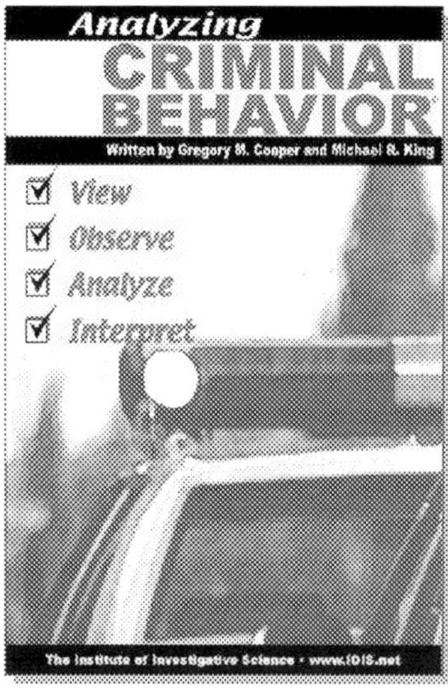

Analyzing Criminal Behavior

Copyright © 2001 by Gregory M. Cooper and Michael R. King

IQ Design Publishing, (801) 698-2750

International Standard Book Number: 0-615-11937-9

Library of Congress Catalog Card Number: Pending/Submitted

First Edition Printing: July 2001
Second Edition Printing: November 2001

ISBN 0-615-11937-9

PRINTED IN THE UNITED STATES OF AMERICA

Dedicated to the Enforcers,
and the victims they serve… living or deceased.

You are the only advocate for justice that the victim has!

About the authors:

Gregory M. Cooper

Gregory M. Cooper is the Provo City Police Chief and Board Chairman of the Utah criminal Tracking and Analysis Project, UTAP. Cooper was employed by the Federal Bureau of Investigation, serving in various investigative and supervisory positions, including the Critical Incident Response Group, FBI Academy, Quantico VA. He served as national manager of the Violent Criminal Apprehension Program (VICAP); supervisor of the Investigative Support Unit and FBI Academy Instructor of Criminal Psychology, Criminal Investigative Analysis and Analytical Aspects of Criminal Behavior.

Cooper co-authored the <u>Crime Classification Manual,</u> (Lexington Press, 1992). He has consulted internationally with law enforcement agencies on over 1,000 cases, including homicides, rapes, kidnaping, product tampering, extortion, political corruption, arson and bombing, workplace violence, stalking and false allegations.

Cooper is an expert witness in crime scene analysis. He has provided expert testimony which behaviorally linked multiple homicides from separate jurisdictions contributing to the conviction of a serial killer. This case is highlighted in the *New York Times* best seller, <u>Mind Hunter,</u> (Douglas, Olshaker, Simon & Schuster), 1995. He is an international speaker and consultant and is an active member of the International Association of Chiefs of Police, Utah Police Chiefs Association, and Academy of Criminal Justice Sciences and has appeared on national and international news and documentary programs.

Michael R. King

Michael R. King is a Lieutenant with the Utah Attorney General's Office and Director of the Utah criminal Tracking and Analysis Project. King is a member and 2002 Chair of the FBI Violent Criminal Apprehension Program National Advisory Board.

Mike began his law enforcement career in 1979 and has served in Patrol, Motors, Tactical Squad/SWAT and Investigations. In 1987, he joined the Weber County Attorney's Office and was the lead investigator in the Zion Society prosecution of 150 individuals practicing bizarre religious beliefs and sexually abusing children. Twelve defendants were charged and convicted in what is considered to be one of the largest, most successfully prosecuted cases of organized cultic abuse in U.S. history.

In 1993, King joined the Attorney General's Office investigating ritual crimes statewide. He has investigated hundreds of ritual and cult crimes and developed investigative protocols as well as authoring the manual, <u>Ritual Crime in Utah</u>. He is the former Chief of Staff to Attorney General Jan Graham who served from 1993-2001 and is co-chair of the Strategic Planning Committee for Utah Law Enforcement. Mike teaches Criminal Investigative Analysis for the Utah Peace Officers Standards and Training academy and as an adjunct faculty member at the Salt Lake Community College. He is published in the <u>FBI Journal,</u> and <u>Police Product News</u>. He is the recipient of the 1989 National Police Officer of the Year award and various other awards and is a featured speaker and trainer nationally. He has consulted in criminal cases worldwide and has appeared on national and international news and documentary programs.

table of contents

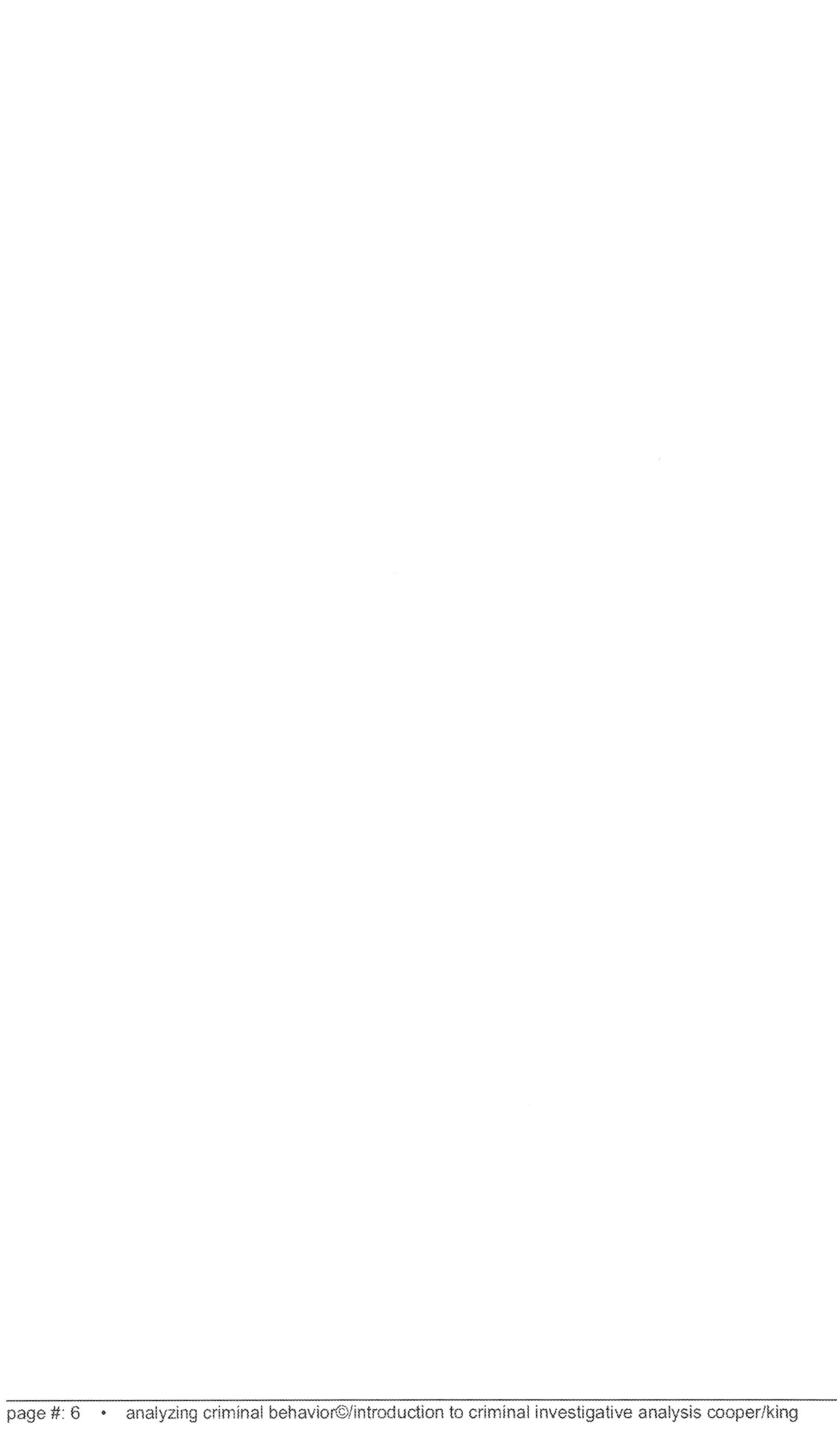

- chapter one -

INTRODUCTION TO
CRIMINAL INVESTIGATIVE ANALYSIS

In the spring of 1986, fear struck the city of Ogden, Utah as the news of a serial rapist made its way through the community of 70,000 residents. Ogden is nestled in the Rocky Mountains approximately 35 miles north of the State of Utah's capital city, Salt Lake. Ogden is the largest community within the 200,000 population of Weber County. Ogden's Police Department employs approximately 120 full-time, sworn police officers, making up more than 25 percent of all the police officers in the county.

The citizens of Ogden earn an average annual wage of $34,000. The largest employers in the area are the federal government installations of Hill Air Force Base and the United States Internal Revenue Service center. The largest civilian employer is the State of Utah. An early railroad town made famous during the rough and tumble days of the 1930's, 1940's and 1950's, Ogden served as a hub to the railroad and was internationally known for 25th Street. 25th Street, sometimes referred to as "two-bit" street because it served as a home to a large number of bars, gambling houses and prostitution, was extremely active and was an area with a high

crime rate. By the close of 1960 though, Ogden had cleaned up the majority of its "vice" problems. As the railroad gave way to air travel, Ogden became like many other western cities. Crime was not rampant, but certainly occurred, reminiscent of the "old" days.

The serial rapist who prowled the streets of Ogden was described as being a white male who was around 30 years old. He had an average build, both in weight and height. One by one in the early morning hours, the rapist terrorized nearly one dozen female victims. His method of operation involved silent entry into the home of a sleeping victim, usually through an unlocked door or open window. His victims were single or divorced women who lived alone, or who had small children in the home. He often confused his victims by calling them by name, a tactic he developed by looking through the victims' mail. He told them that he had been watching them for some time and that he knew where they worked. On several occasions he told them he was a police officer and that he would know if they ever reported him.

During his crime spree over several years, the predator, who soon gained fame as the "Ogden Serial Rapist," was identified in nine rapes, twenty residential burglaries and dozens of voyeurism complaints in the city. In reality, he was committing similar crimes in communities throughout an eleven-state region. Eventually, the "Ogden Serial Rapist," who worked as a long-haul truck driver, admitted to raping over 80 women. He confessed to hundreds of business and residential burglaries and admitted to stealing hundreds of thousands of dollars worth of property, drugs and currency.

At this same time, two other rapists were hunting for victims in and along the streets of Ogden. One of the predators was arrested after committing several assaults and the community and police thought they had captured their offender and they began to settle back into their feeling of security. To the amazement of the police and the community, the rapes continued. Questions arose regarding the validity of the arrest of the first offender. Some wondered if the rapes were being committed by a single perpetrator or whether there may be "copy-cat" predators working the streets.

Several months later, another perpetrator was captured. This offender was much different in the manner in which he surprised and maintained control over his victims. The differences were peculiar and enabled law enforcement officers to differentiate between the three predators. As investigators studied the assaults and the way the offenders gained control over their victims, patterns emerged.

Those patterns led investigators to a strategy which ultimately ended in the arrest and conviction of all three offenders. Eventually, the predators were tried and found guilty in a court of law. Today, they reside in a correctional facility in the State of Utah.

"Criminal investigative analysis," also termed "criminal profiling" or "psychological profiling," is the process of reviewing and assessing the behavioral facts of a violent criminal act from a law enforcement and/or investigative perspective. It includes interpreting the offender's behavior and interaction with the victim displayed during the commission of the crimes and the significance of interdependent behavioral elements.

Just as investigators in the "Ogden Serial Rapist" case discovered the unique behaviors that the offender displayed as he communicated with his victims verbally, non-verbally and sexually, the process of criminal investigative analysis looks closely at criminal cases from a behavioral perspective, not just the forensic or eye-witness angle most commonly used. In the first Ogden case, investigators learned that if the offender was denied oral sex during the course of a rape, he would attempt another rape within a few hours. Once this fact was discovered, investigators began asking the victims about the sequence of events during each assault.

Once they determined that this criteria had been met, they "called out the troops." Within  minutes of a failed rape, dozens of police officers crawled the streets of Ogden and, fortunately, the "Ogden Serial Rapist" was apprehended as he fled the scene of his primary target.

Accurate interpretation of these behavioral clues can assist law enforcement officers in identifying a motive and formulating the characteristics of the "imaginary suspect," thus supplementing their efforts in *leading* the investigation, rather than *reacting* to it. The effective application of criminal investigative analysis techniques provides essential services to law enforcement, security officers, mental health professionals, prosecutors and many other professions and disciplines. Behavior truly is the universal language, and when properly diagnosed can help us in solving crimes, addressing psychological and behavioral problems, and efficiently managing people.

The example of the "Ogden Serial Rapist" is an excellent one when examining the benefits of criminal investigative analysis. Some additional types of offenses or incidents in which criminal investigative analysis has been effective include cases of homicide, arson, autoerotic death, bombing, equivocal death, espionage, extortion, infant abduction, kidnaping, missing persons, product tampering, public corruption, ritualistic crime, sexual victimization of children, stalking, terrorism and white-collar crime.

Throughout this book, and in the course study of criminal investigative analysis, we will discuss behavioral analysis, offender characteristics, motive identification, crime scene analysis, signature assessment, and recidivism.

Police officers, sheriffs' deputies, state troopers and federal agents all attend the training academy when they are first hired. In the academy, they

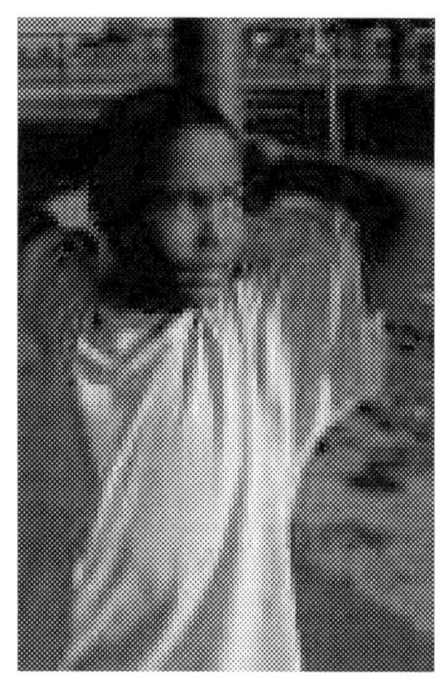

are taught the basics of law enforcement. They learn about the laws of their particular state and nation. They receive training in firearms and arrest control tactics. They attend classes where they learn how to handle situations ranging from domestic violence to traffic enforcement. Unfortunately, the majority of investigators across the country learn the art of interview and interrogation, forensics and case management through the process of "OJT," or on-the-job-training. Seldom is an new investigator prepared to handle the emotional stress associated with a crime of violence where bizarre physical or sexual assault occurs.

Each year thousands of crimes of violence are committed across the United States and abroad. These crimes often include bizarre verbal, nonverbal and sexual overtones. Through the process of behavioral analysis, the investigator can enhance his/her investigative abilities and increase the chance of apprehending the offender. Through the process of identifying the many variables in these complex types of cases, we can more quickly gain an understanding of the offender's motivation for the crime, the process used in selecting a victim and the manner in which the offender avoids detection.

We are experiencing crime at an alarming rate: a murder in our country occurs every 34 minutes; a forcible rape every 6 minutes; every 1 minute a robbery occurs; and every 27 seconds a motor vehicle is stolen. One Crime Index Offense occurs every 3 seconds and the numbers go on and on. (FBI, Uniform Crime Report of 1999, published by the Department of Justice Administration)

While the "Crime Clock" illustrates how many crimes occur each second and minute nationwide, it does not include cases of missing persons or unidentified bodies. Current statistics indicate that thousands of people are reported missing each year in the United States. Thousands more unidentified bodies are discovered that cannot be linked to any of the reported missing cases. These figures, along with some of the other challenges that are faced today, will be discussed in the following chapters.

What we've learned is this: law enforcement can no longer afford the luxury of relying on forensics, eye witnesses, circumstantial evidence or confessions to solve crimes. We must improve our ability to assess criminal behavior and use that tool to predict and reduce crime.

2000 Crime Clock

one *MURDER* *every 33.9 minutes*	one *CRIME INDEX OFFENSE* *every 2.7 seconds*
one *FORCIBLE RAPE* *every 5.8 minutes*	one *PROPERTY CRIME* *every 3.1 seconds*
one *ROBBERY* *every 1.3 minutes*	one *LARCENY-THEFT* *every 4.5 seconds*
one *MOTOR VEHICLE THEFT* *every 27.1 seconds*	one *AGGRAVATED ASSAULT* *every 34.6 seconds*
one *VIOLENT CRIME* *every 22.1 seconds*	one *BURGLARY* *every 15.4 seconds*

Chapter Review

Define "Criminal Investigative Analysis."

The process of reviewing & assessing the behavioral facts of a violent crime from a law enforcement/ investigative perspective

In this chapter, rape was the crime where Criminal Investigative Analysis (CIA) proved useful. Name six additional areas where CIA has proven beneficial.

1. ~~offender characteristics~~ arson   2. kidnapping

3. extortion   4. espionage

5. bombing   6. stalking

What does the "Crime Clock" tell us about the problems being faced in criminal investigations?

cannot use forensics, testimony, eyewitness, confessions or circumstantial evidence to solve crimes

- chapter two -

CURRENT CHALLENGES

Abstract

Law enforcement efforts around the globe are focused on protecting life and property. While this mission remains the same from one geographic region to the next, enforcement agencies are facing many challenges as they try to accomplish this great responsibility. This chapter will look at some of those challenges and the "proactive" strategies being employed to combat them.

Criminal investigative analysis, or behavioral profiling, increases the success, quality and speed of the criminal justice process from the crime scene to the courtroom. Further application of these principles will aid in the communication efforts of thousands of agencies across the United States.

According to information obtained from the Utah Department of Public Safety in 1998, there are nearly 104,000 people who are reported missing each year in our country. Another 3,900 unidentified bodies are recovered annually which cannot be linked to those people who are reported missing. The FBI Uniform Crime Reports for 1980 to 1999 indicate that we are averaging over 20,907 homicides each year for the past 20 years. That alone represents 418,113 people who were murdered – that's more people than the total population of cities the size of Las Vegas, Nevada or Sacramento, California. (Source: Population Division, U.S. Census Bureau, SU-99-1)

Let's do the math! If ninety percent of all the missing people in the world made it back home (which seems very optimistic), then over 10,400 are still unaccounted for each year. Add that figure to the 3,900 unidentified bodies found each year, and the 20,907 homicides, and law enforcement has 35,207 dead or missing bodies that require investigation.

In 1999, 69% of all homicides were cleared compared to 79% in 1976 and 90% in the 1960's. Homicide has the highest clearance rate of all serious crimes. (Bureau of Justice Statistics of Homicide Trends in the U.S., 1999 report)

"Cleared" refers to the situation when a law enforcement agency arrests a person who is charged with an offense and turned over to the court for prosecution, or when a case is cleared by exceptional means such as when an identified offender is killed during apprehension or commits suicide.

If America's law enforcement agencies fail to share information, cooperate in investigations or coordinate intelligence information, we are yielding the "upper hand" to the perpetrators of crime. From time to time, in major criminal investigations such as the "Night Stalker" of California, law enforcement officers from multiple cities, counties or state and federal agencies come together to form "Task Forces" to combat the problem. History has proven that when this cooperative effort occurs, the crimes are more quickly solved.

In 1997 in the State of Utah, the chiefs and sheriffs, operating under the Strategic Planning Committee for Utah Law Enforcement discussed the formation of an on-going task force made up of volunteers who could provide expertise, suggestions, recommendations and investigation of complex criminal cases. The finished product became known as UTAP, the Utah criminal Tracking and Analysis Project. UTAP is the brainchild of Provo City Police Chief Greg Cooper and Utah Attorney General's Office Lieutenant Mike King.

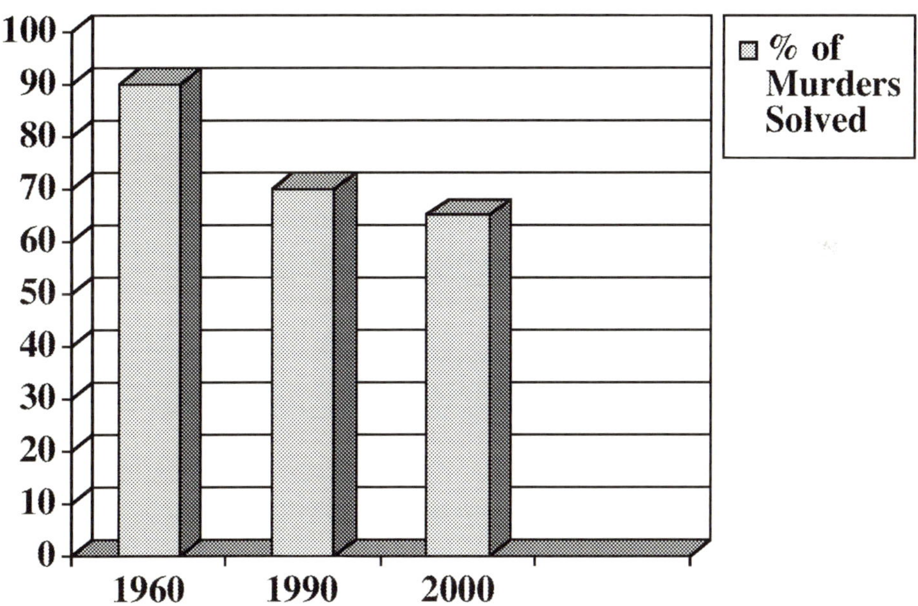

**Percentage of Homicides Solved
by Year**

Bureau of Justice Statistics of Homicide Trends in the U.S., 1999 report

UTAP: Utah criminal Tracking and Analysis Project

Director: Lieutenant Mike King
Utah Attorney General's Office
(801) 698-2750

Chairman: Chief Greg Cooper
Provo Police Department
(801) 852-6037

The UTAP mission is similar to the FBI's ViCAP (Violent Criminal Apprehension Program) regarding the facilitation of cooperation, communication and coordination between law enforcement agencies. The services provided by UTAP are strictly supportive in nature and will be initiated exclusively at the prompting of the requesting agency. Additionally, services will be offered primarily in the form of suggestions, recommendations, observations and references based upon a review and analysis of cases presented by submitting agencies. Moreover, while UTAP is housed within and a project of the Utah Attorney General's Office in Salt Lake City, Utah, its analytical function is independent of any federal, state, county or city government. Recipient agencies are free to accept or refuse the services provided by UTAP, which is a board consisting of consultants with multidimensional expertise and multi-agency representation.

It is the intent of UTAP to provide assistance to any legitimate law enforcement agency confronted with unusual, bizarre and/or repetitive violent crime. Through the expertise of its staff of crime analysts, sociologists, forensic scientists, political scientists, computer scientists and police specialists, UTAP brings a multi-disciplinary approach to a wide variety of investigative problems. UTAP is prepared to provide several types of crime analysis assistance to state, county, and city law enforcement agencies, without charge.

UTAP may conduct a crime analysis of particular crimes for several purposes. Criminal investigative analysis (CIA) is simply a tool for law enforcement to assist in the solution of unsolved crimes. It involves a method of reviewing and assessing the facts of a criminal act by individuals who have investigative experience and specialized academic training. It often includes interpreting the offender's behavior and interaction with the victim, as exhibited during the commission of the crime or as evidenced by the subsequent crime scene. CIA should be viewed as a process of reviewing crime(s) from a law enforcement perspective. The various products or services which might result from an analysis are as follows:

Crime Analysis:

An independent analyst, who is uncluttered with various on-scene stresses and extraneous information, reviews initial crime scene information and preliminary investigative efforts. Possible motives may be detected as well as a determination of the sequence of the events which occurred during the offense. Multiple crimes can be reviewed to determine if the same offender was involved, and suggestions can be offered that may help direct the course of an investigation. The case may also be classified using categories set forth in the Crime Classification Manual (Lexington Press, 1992).

Profiles of Unknown Offenders:

By analyzing the way a crime was committed, investigative profilers can identify the major personality and behavioral characteristics of an individual. Generally, the person's basic patterns of behavior exhibited in commission of a crime will also be present in that person's lifestyle. Thus, an investigative analysis may be able to determine the type of person who committed the crime and the possible motive(s) for the crime. Some, but not necessarily all, of the following areas may be addressed in a typical profile:

Personality Assessment:

This type of analysis identifies a suspect's strengths, weaknesses, and vulnerabilities from a law enforcement perspective. Identifying these strengths and weaknesses can assist the investigator in preparing for and conducting an interview. The information gained may also provide insight into the subject's motivation for the crime and assist the investigator in gaining a better understanding of the offender's reasons for committing the crime.

Because each request is unique, the assessment process requires a detailed submission of data about the person targeted and demands extensive review and consultation by the analyst. The availability of this material is considered essential to constructing appropriate interview strategies.

Interview Techniques:

This service combines a personality assessment with an analysis of the crime and the behavior exhibited therein. Suggestions are made as how best to interview a subject, particularly when the agency may only have one opportunity for a successful interview. These techniques may include suggestions on the most appropriate type of interview, desired approach, and the best environment in which to conduct the interview. Studies have shown that certain types of offenders are more apt to feel comfortable or threatened based on the type and manner of interview technique. Utilizing the appropriate approach can make the defining difference in obtaining a confession or having an interview prematurely terminated.

Likewise, the location of the interview can lend to the success of the interrogation. Some interviews may need to be conducted in the controlled environment of a police station by investigators who represent a great deal of authority. In other circumstances, a quiet interview in an offender's home or place of work may prove to be the best strategy.

Investigative Suggestions:

These suggestions may be offered based on the evaluation of the crime scene and the assessment of the offender. The suggestions might range from conducting additional interviews, to gathering and testing additional pieces of evidence. Other suggestions may deal with interview strategies, media campaigns or accessing of outside disciplines.

Prosecutive and Trial Strategies:

This service may be provided at the request of either the investigative agency or prosecuting attorney, and can involve recommendations to include:

Considerations regarding jury selection

Possible cross-examination techniques for offender and/or witnesses (will require personality assessments)

Overall prosecutive theme development

Crime analysis / crime motivation

Threat Analysis:

When verbal or written communications are received, this service will attempt to determine if the same author is responsible for the communications and/or whether the author has the intent, knowledge or means to carry out the threats. A behavioral description of the author may be provided to assist in identification and apprehension. In light of the many national and local tragedies that have occurred by both domestic and foreign terrorists, this service is one of the most valuable yet least used of all of UTAP's services.

Search Warrant Assistance:

A major component of criminal investigative analysis is research which has shown that certain behavior and personality traits are commonly possessed by specific types of offenders (i.e., child molesters). This information can be highly beneficial in search warrant affidavits in order to describe the types of evidence that can be expected to be found (i.e., souvenirs from victims; seemingly innocuous items which may have evidentiary value). Timeliness (staleness) issues might be alleviated through the appropriate use of data gained from current research.

Forensic Assistance:

One of the most difficult areas for police investigators to understand is that of forensic evidence. Very few officers have sufficient technical training to properly interpret bloodstain patterns, DNA results, etc. This service will provide help in determining which analytical tools would be most beneficial and who to call for the best advice. Areas of expertise include fingerprint analysis, firearms identification, trace evidence (hairs, fibers, soil, etc.), blood, and other physiological and scene reconstruction.

Criminal Justice Databases:

Nearly all law enforcement agencies have access to state of the art technology and computer databases to assist them. AFIS, CODIS, NCIC, DRUGFIRE, and ULEIN offer on-line search capability that can greatly enhance an investigation. This booklet will discuss briefly many of these databases.

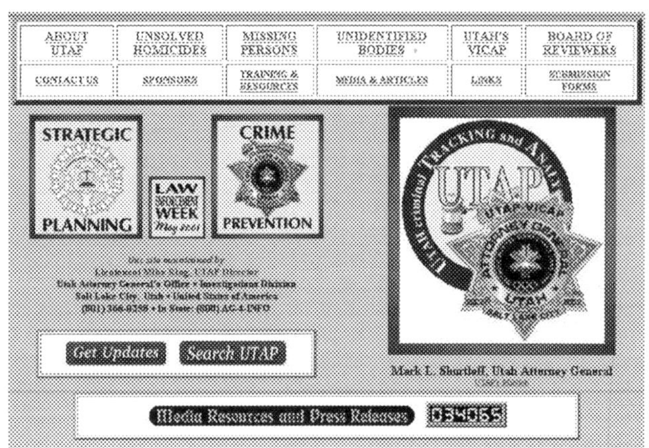

Expert Testimony:

Occasionally, successful prosecutive strategies incorporate the use of expert witness testimony in support of case presentation. UTAP will maintain a reference base to assist any agency in identifying possible resources.

Additional UTAP Services:

UTAP has proven its value time and again with investigators from Utah and across the nation. In addition to the analytical services provided, UTAP provides: *Cutting-edge training, not only in crimes against persons, but financial crimes and threat assessment; a webpage that is accessible to law enforcement and the general public. (The purpose of the webpage is to solicit information from the public on unsolved homicides, unidentified bodies and missing persons where foul play is suspected. The page can be accessed at: www.UTAP.org); creative resourcing of investigative needs to take advantage of public and private opportunities; and strategies in policing.* There are a series of forms that can be obtained through UTAP by mail or via the internet. They are:

Mission Statements and Criminal Investigative Analysis Services Application

Types of Cases Suitable for Analysis

Submission Forms and Instructions

Submission Chart/Overview

Instructions

Submission Materials Needed

Attachments Overview

Report Heading Sheets

Resource Materials

Questioning the Rape Victim for Offender Behavior

Submission Chart

✔ = Should be included
★ = Include if exists

CIA: Criminal Investigative Analysis

	(Explained on page ___)	Homicide/ Sexual Homicide	Sexual Assault	Child Molestation /Abduction	Equivocal Death	Kidnapping/ Extortion	Arson/ Bombing	Other	Other
NARRATIVE SECTION									
Overall synopsis	1	✔	✔	✔	✔	✔	✔		
Description of area	1	✔	✔	✔	✔	✔	✔		
Crime scene description	2	✔	✔	★	✔	★	✔		
Summary of victimology	2	✔	✔	✔	✔	✔	★		
Summary of medical reports	2	✔	✔	★	✔				
Summary of other testing	2	★	★	★	★	★	★		
Similar crimes statement	2	✔	✔	✔	✔	✔	✔		
Summary of media coverage	2	✔	✔	✔	✔	✔	✔		
Miscellaneous	2	★	★	★	★	★	★		
Whether suspects exist	2	✔	✔	✔	✔	✔	✔		
ATTACHMENTS									
A. Investigative reports	3	✔	✔	✔	✔	✔	✔		
B. Maps (points of interest keyed)	3	✔	✔	✔	✔	✔	✔		
C. ViCAP Form	3	★	★	★	★	★	★		
D. Crime scene sketch	3	✔	★	★	✔	★	✔		
E. Medical Reports	3	✔	✔	★	✔	★			
F. Forensic test results	3	★	★	★	★	★	★		
G. Victimology information	3	✔	✔	✔	✔	✔	★		
H. Media coverage	4	★	★	★	★	★	★		
I. PHOTOS - Crime scene(s)	4	✔	★	★	✔	★	✔		
J. PHOTOS - Victim prior to crime	4	✔	✔	✔	✔	✔			
K. PHOTOS - Medical/autopsy	4	✔	★	★	✔				
L. Suspect information (enclose in sealed envelope)	4	★	★	★	★	★	★		
M. Miscellaneous	4	★	★	★	★	★	★		

Questioning the Sexual Assault Victim for Offender Behavior

Background Information / Victim Associate of Victim / Interview

Victim Data Form

Equivocal Death Questions

Offender Characteristics Worksheet

Victimology Assessment

Deposit / Discovery Site

Medical Examiner's Report / Forensic Information

Crime Assessment Scenario / Crime Scene Scenario

Behavior Indicators / Innocent vs. Others
Critical Questions that can Assist in Detection of Deception

Interrogation

Why People Confess/Don't Confess

Personality Assessment Questions

Personality Characteristics

Rapist Typology

Sexual Assault Worksheet

Utah Attorney General's Office
Utah *criminal* **Tracking and Analysis Project**
Webpage Submission Form

Return completed form to: Lieutenant Mike King
Utah Attorney General's Office
236 State Capitol, Salt Lake City, Utah 84114
(801) 366-0258 • Fax: (801) 366-0242 • email: Mike@UTAP.org

Submitting Agency:	**TYPE OF SUBMISSION:**
Address:	
City/State/Zip:	☐ **Unsolved Homicide**
Contact Person:	
Telephone Number:	☐ **Unidentified Body**
Fax Number:	
Email Address:	☐ **Missing Person**
Date of Case/Discovery:	(Foulplay suspected)
County of Case/Discovery	

How would you like the investigator notified of tips or information. (preferential is email):
☐ Email   ☐ Telephone   ☐ Fax

Short description of events as you would like the information to appear on the website:

____
____
____
____
____
____
____
____
____
____
____

use additional sheets if necessary

VICTIM INFORMATION

Name: ___________________

DOB: ____________ Race: ______

Sex: ☐ Male ☐ Female

Ht.: ______ Wt.: ______

Hair: __________ Eyes: __________

WOULD YOU LIKE HELP WITH THE VICAP SUBMISSION?
☐ YES ☐ NO

*Send a **Color Photo of Victim** while alive. You can mail the photo and it will be returned. Scanned photo's preferred (.jpg), along with any other photo's you would like on the website. Please Email photo to:* Mike@UTAP.org

Examples can be found at:
www.UTAP.org

Submissions to UTAP can be made via the internet, regular mail service, drop off or over the phone. Specific case information for each submission to the UTAP site is controlled by the agency. A photograph of the victim and any additional photographs depicting the crime scene, elements of the crime, etc., that are in good taste are entered on the site.

The UTAP-ViCAP Connection

In March of 2000, the Utah Attorney General's Office accepted the FBI's request to serve as the lead agency for ViCAP in the State of Utah. Under this agreement, the UAG's Office serves as the statewide coordinator and clearinghouse for all Utah cases involving Unsolved Homicides, Missing Persons (where foul play is suspected) and Unidentified Bodies.

Police agencies from across the state will upload their cases to the AG's case analysts, who will compare with similar cases. If similarities are discovered, the AG's Office will notify the agencies involved and encourage their cooperation with one another.

The Attorney General's Office will forward all Utah-based cases to the national database housed at the FBI National Academy in Quantico, VA. Once there, members of the FBI will compare Utah cases against cases from across the nation and participating countries.

RMIN: Rocky Mountain Information Network

The Rocky Mountain Information Network provides intelligence services such as database checks, state and local intelligence checks, drivers license checks and photo acquisition, criminal history checks, ACIC and NCIC warrants checks as well as these additional checks:

    Vehicle, boat, pilot and plane
    Telephone subscriber information
    Utility information
    Corporate and business information
    Postal service information
    Credit applications

Interpol and Immigration
NICB and RAIN checks

RMIN has secured access, only available through RISSGATE (http://
rmin.riss.net) where they can do online inquiries, gang research and provide
valuable forms and publications. The analytical services section can provide
telephone record analysis, link, case, visual investigative and financial
analysis. RMIN's experts can assist with computer forensics, court charts and
analytical training.

RMIN also provides training assistance, agency referrals, patch call
assistance and a monthly intelligence bulletin. RMIN services are available
free of charge to member agencies. UTAP will pay for the first year of
membership for agencies who are not members. (Contact UTAP for more
information.) Investigators can receive assistance locating information on:

Individuals
Addresses
Vehicles
Businesses
Subscriber information
Log Scanning/NCIC off-line searches
Firearms
Employment histories
Military records
Licensing
Vital records
Court records
Networking assistance
Gang intelligence
Property information

Utah Department of Corrections
Corrections F-Track:

Law Enforcement personnel can access Corrections offender data through the Bureau of Criminal Identification (BCI) Rap Sheet. When a Rap Sheet is pulled, BCI includes data about the offender's current status with Corrections. Access can also be obtained through Corrections web site where authorized personnel can obtain data on offenders. Direct logons to the F-track data base have been established for read only access to large parts of the information in the system. This method of access requires DOC staff to install the F-track software on the user's computer, so the ability to grant it is limited. Utah DOC probation and parole offices will also provide data from the data base over the telephone to authorized personnel.

Utah Department of Corrections Sex Offender Registry

Law Enforcement personnel can access the Registry through the DOC web site. Additional information on sex offenders can be obtained by calling the Adult Probation and Parole headquarters office. Utah Code Ann. 77-27-21.5, Sex Offender Registration, requires the Utah Department of Corrections to develop, operate, and maintain a registry of persons who have either been convicted of or entered a plea in abeyance to certain sex offenses. Those offenses are listed here and in subsection (1)(d) of the statute.

Agg. Exploitation of Prostitution : 76-10-1306
Lewdness Involving a Child : 76-9-702.5
Sexual Exploitation of a Minor : 76-5a-3
Sex Abuse of & Agg Sexual Abuse of a Child: 76-5-404.1

Forcible Sexual Abuse : 76-5-404

Forcible Sodomy : 76-5-403

Sodomy on a Child : 76-5-403.1

Incest : 76-7-102

Rape of a Child : 76-5-402.1

Object Rape : 76-5-402.2

Object Rape of a Child : 76-5-402.3

Child Kidnapping : 76-5-301.1

Aggravated Sexual Assault : 76-5-405

Unlawful Sexual Activity w/a Minor : 76-5-401

Sexual Abuse of a Minor : 76-5-401.1

Unlawful Sexual Conduct w/a 16-17 yr old : 76-5-401.2

Rape 76-5-402

Registration is also required of individuals who are committed to the Utah State Hospital by reason of their mental condition and who also have committed or been alleged to have committed any of the listed offenses. Section 77-27-21.5 mandates the Department to disseminate to the public all information in the registry. The Department chooses to meet this demand via this website. By placing registry information on the Internet, the Utah Department of Corrections makes no representation, either implied or expressed, that all information is accurate. Though much of the information is of record, some is gathered from the offenders themselves, who are required to list their addresses whenever they move as well as annually. The information contained on this site does not imply listed individuals will commit a specific type of crime in the future, nor does it imply that if a future crime is committed by a listed individual what the nature of that crime may be. The Department makes no representation as to any offender's likelihood of re-offending.

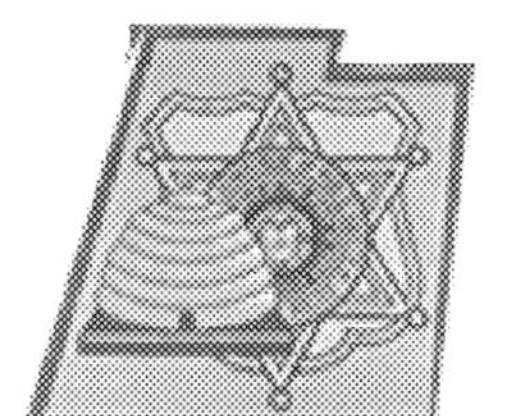

ULEIN: Utah Law Enforcement Information Network

The Utah Law Enforcement Information Network (ULEIN) is a statewide criminal intelligence database containing over 130,000 records, a motor vehicle registration search and a case management system. The major goal of the ULEIN project is to help facilitate intelligence and information sharing between the various law enforcement agencies throughout Utah. The ULEIN system is currently utilized by 550 active users representing virtually every law enforcement agency in the State of Utah and is available to any law enforcement agency that wishes to use it free of charge.

ViCAP: Violent Criminal Apprehension Program

In 1985, the Federal Bureau of Investigation announced the birth of ViCAP, (Violent Criminal Apprehension Program). The purpose of ViCAP is to provide a national clearinghouse for law enforcement agencies to coordinate information on missing persons, unidentified bodies, and homicides. Participation in the program is voluntary and is available to all law enforcement agencies in the country. It was determined that a significant number of cases bearing common characteristics could be identified by collating these categories of data.

ViCAP's mission is to facilitate cooperation, communication, and coordination between law enforcement agencies and provide support in their efforts to investigate, identify, track, apprehend, and prosecute violent serial offenders. ViCAP is a nationwide data information center designed to collect, collate, and analyze crimes of violence - specifically murder. Cases examined by ViCAP include:

> *Solved or unsolved homicides or attempts, especially those that involve an abduction; are apparently random, motiveless, or sexually oriented; or are known or suspected to be part of a series;*
>
> *Missing persons, where the circumstances indicate a strong possibility of foul play and the victim is still missing; and,*
>
> *Unidentified dead bodies where the manner of death is known or suspected to be homicide.*

Currently, the ViCAP National Advisory Board is working toward implementation of a Sexual Assault component for the ViCAP tracking system. It is anticipated that ViCAP will begin to maintain data on bizarre sexual assaults sometime in the year 2003.

For ViCAP to work effectively, it needs an invitation from local law enforcement to participate in an investigation. The FBI provides, free of charge, the software to set up the ViCAP database. The program has been embraced by many agencies, with busier operations in cities including Los Angeles, Chicago, Detroit and Dallas. It is also being operated by state organizations like the State of Utah through the Utah Attorney General's Office, UTAP/ViCAP project.

Cases with an arrested or identified offender can be submitted to the ViCAP system by local law enforcement investigators for comparison and possible matching with unsolved cases. Once a case is entered into the ViCAP database, it is compared continually against all other entries on the basis of certain aspects of the crime. The purpose of this is to detect signature aspects of a crime and similar patterns of modus operandi (MO's) which will, in turn, allow ViCAP personnel to pinpoint those crimes that may have been committed by the same offender in other areas of the country. If patterns are found, the ViCAP coordinators will then work with all the law enforcement agencies involved to team up in solving the crimes.

When a pattern of criminal activity is discovered – for example a serial murder suspect has been identified – ViCAP can then assist law enforcement agencies by coordinating a multi-agency investigative conference. The multi-agency conference becomes especially important when the suspect or suspects have traveled throughout the country. A very valuable product of prior conferences was the coordination of activities such as search warrants, interview matters, and laboratory testing.

The VICAP database is effective in solving crimes from the present and the past. Law enforcement officers may enter cases that occurred in the year 2000, the 1980's or even the 1950's; any case that law enforcement feels ViCAP can assist in may be offered.

There are various other databases and organizations that can provide valuable assistance and support to law enforcement investigations. Here is a brief summary of a few of them. It should be noted that the contact information and description of the services were obtained through public documents and are not considered classified in any manner of which the authors are aware.

AFIS or IAFIS: The Integrated Automated Fingerprint Identification System

(IAFIS) Project has its roots in the 1960s and 1970s when the FBI began investigating the feasibility of automating the fingerprint identification process. During that period the Identification Division, predecessor to CJIS, began working with the National Bureau of Standards (now the National Institute for Standards and Technology) to develop algorithms for searching and matching fingerprints using computer technology. In addition, research contracts were awarded for the development of prototype fingerprint scanners and matchers. These prototype scanners and matchers evolved into the Automated Fingerprint Reader System (AFRS).

Instead of using ink and fingerprint cards to take fingerprints of arrested subjects and job applicants, the fingerprint images are captured electronically by scanning the fingers on a live-scan system. The textual information normally found at the top of a fingerprint card (e.g., name, date of birth, arrest information, etc.) is entered on the keyboard of the live-scan system. This textual information, along with the digital fingerprint images are compressed and formatted according to approved standards and transmitted to and through the FBI IAFIS as well as local, state, and regional AFIS. (Taken from the FBI website http://www.fbi.gov/hq/cjisd/iafis.htm), 2001

The ability to search a latent fingerprint against a large database of fingerprint images has proven to be an incredible boon to law enforcement agencies throughout the country. Utah is a participating state in the Western Identification Network (WIN), which stores in a database the fingerprint images of seven (7) western states. WIN will also integrate into the national AFIS system housed at FBI Headquarters in Clarksburg, West Virginia.

Law enforcement agencies desiring a latent fingerprint comparison to these large databases are encouraged to bring the prints to the Crime Laboratory, where the search will be conducted. Latent prints can be submitted to the Crime Lab in the same way any piece of evidence is submitted.

CODIS: Combined DNA Index System

The FBI Laboratory's Combined DNA Index System (CODIS) blends forensic science and computer technology into an effective tool for solving violent crimes. CODIS enables federal, state, and local crime labs to exchange and compare DNA profiles electronically, thereby linking crimes to each other and to convicted offenders.

CODIS began as a pilot project in 1990 serving 14 state and local laboratories. The DNA Identification Act of 1994 (Public Law 103 322) formalized the FBI's authority to establish a national DNA index for law enforcement purposes. In October 1998, the FBI's National DNA Index System (NDIS) became operational. CODIS is implemented as a distributed database with three hierarchical levels (or tiers) - local, state, and national. NDIS is the highest level in the CODIS hierarchy, and enables the laboratories participating in the CODIS Program to exchange and compare DNA profiles on a national level. All DNA profiles originate at the local level (LDIS), then flow to the state (SDIS) and national levels. SDIS allows laboratories within states to exchange DNA profiles. The tiered approach allows state and local agencies to operate their databases according to their specific legislative or legal requirements. (Taken from the FBI web: http://www.fbi.gov/hq/lab/codis/index1.htm), 2001

CODIS is to DNA what AFIS is to fingerprints. Throughout the country, agencies are loading DNA profiles into a database of convicted sexual assault and homicide offenders. In some states, all convicted felons are put into CODIS. Prior to being released from penal institutions, defendants are required to provide a blood sample in order to have a DNA profile put into the CODIS database. Initially, Utah's portion of the database will be approximately 4,000 offenders. A state of Utah search can be conducted and if there are no hits locally, then a nationwide search can be initiated.

The CODIS database is expected to provide law enforcement with an excellent resource of information leading to the capture of repeat offenders. CODIS searches are done by personnel at the state Crime Lab/DNA Section.

EPIC: El Paso Intelligence Center

EPIC stands for the El Paso Intelligence Center located in El Paso, Texas. EPIC is operated as a Drug Enforcement Administration (DEA) led intelligence center. EPIC is made up of several participating federal agencies: Immigration & Naturalization Service (INS), US Customs Service, FBI, Bureau of Alcohol, Tobacco, & Firearms (ATF), as well as the US Marshals Service, Departments of State & Interior, the Internal Revenue Service (IRS), US Secret Service (USSS), National Security Agency (NSA), US Coast Guard, the Federal Aviation Administration (FAA), Federal Highway Administration, and the US Border Patrol (USBP); and two state agencies, Texas Department of Public Safety and the Texas Air National Guard. These are not the only agencies that are members of EPIC. All 50 states, the Bureau of Prisons, AMTRAK, the District of Columbia, Puerto Rico, American Samoa, Guam, Virgin Islands, and the Royal Canadian Mounted Police (RCMP) are called Associate Member Agencies.

EPIC can provide the following information : information on drug and weapons trafficking, as well as alien smuggling port of entry information on vehicles, aircraft, vessels, commercial cargo, and shipping container lookouts.

Other services are intelligence support, 24/7 watch operation for rapid dissemination of all information and has the ability to post a variety of alerts and lookouts (national and international) for suspects If you need more information you can contact EPIC at their main number.

FINCEN: Financial Crimes Enforcement Network

FINCEN is operated by the US Department of the Treasury. It serves as a link between law enforcement, financial and commercial databases. Through its "Project Gateway" program, FINCEN works with law enforcement in each state so they have on-line access to FINCEN's databases. These gateways, with their cutting edge technology, allow each state direct electronic access to financial information. Inquiries can obtain information regarding:

Banking Information filed under the Bank Secrecy Act (BSA), including Currency Transaction Report (CTR) and Casinos (CTRC), International Transportation of Currency or Monetary Instruments (CMIR), Report of Foreign Bank & Financial Accounts (FBAR), and Suspicious Activity Report (SAR).

Access to federal databases operated by the Treasury Bureaus, Drug Enforcement Administration (DEA), Department of Defense (DOD), and the Postal Inspection Service. Access to commercial databases, which can provide information regarding asset ownership, links between individuals, businesses, and assets, as well as locate individuals.

INTERPOL: International Criminal Police Organization

INTERPOL is the International Criminal Police Organization with national central bureaus (NCB's) in its 177 member nations. INTERPOL maintains a global communications network to help coordinate international criminal investigations among its member countries. The NCB's function as a point of contact for international law enforcement; the United States National Central Bureau (USNCB) of INTERPOL is operated by the US Attorney General, under the direction of the Departments of Justice and Treasury. INTERPOL can provide information such as address verifications, criminal records checks, disaster victim ID/ humanitarian requests (Death notifications, etc.) APB's (All Points Bulletins) and witness interviews, trace and locate services, missing persons, abducted children, telephone subscriber information, weapons and vehicle traces and assistance in the location of stolen arts and artifacts.

All inquiries from federal agencies should be made in accordance with established departmental policies. State and local law enforcement officers need to contact their State Liaison Office. It should be noted that USNCB has access to the TECS database, as well as NCIC and the National Center for Missing and Exploited Children. More information on what is specifically required for filing a "Request for International Assistance" can be found at the USNCB's website: www.usdoj.gov/usncb

LEIU: Law Enforcement Intelligence Unit

LEIU is the Law Enforcement Intelligence Unit overseen by the California Department of Justice. Its

membership consists of over 250 agencies in the United States, Canada, Australia, and South Africa. Some of the information that can be provided to its members is confidential organized crime & gang information, intelligence network of organized crime & gang professionals worldwide, professional criminal intelligence standards & guidelines, training seminars on criminal intelligence, organized crime, & terrorism, gaming license information and assistance in developing a criminal intelligence unit.

 ## DEA: Drug Enforcement Administration

The Drug Enforcement Administration maintains information on individuals and businesses licensed to handle narcotics and persons in violation of federal drug law and regulations. DEA administers EPIC and NADDIS.

 ## NADDIS: Narcotics and Dangerous Drug Information System

For more information see the DEA website at: www.doj.gov/dea

NADDIS, the Narcotics and Dangerous Drug Information System, is maintained by the DEA. It is a database that contains over 3 million records, and can provide information on narcotics-related cases or files, smugglers of funds, other contraband, and aliens. Access is limited to DEA agents or through EPIC. Inquiries should be made through your local DEA office or through the DEA Task Force representative, associated with your department.

NCIC: National Crime Information Center

The purpose for maintaining the NCIC system is to provide a computerized database for ready access by a criminal justice agency making an inquiry and for prompt disclosure of information in the system from other criminal justice agencies about crimes and criminals. This information assists authorized agencies in criminal justice and related law enforcement objectives, such as apprehending fugitives, locating missing persons, locating and returning stolen property, as well as in the protection of the law enforcement officers encountering the individuals described in the system.

This database, operated by the Federal Bureau of Investigations (FBI), provides information on Wanted Persons, Stolen Property, Stolen, Missing, or Recovered Gun Information, Stolen License Plates, Criminal History Checks, Stolen/Wanted Vehicles (Auto, Boat, Aircraft, Motorcycles), Stolen, Embezzled, Missing, or Counterfeited Securities, Bonds, Stocks, and Currency. NCIC can be accessed directly through NLETS or by visiting them on the web at: http://foia.fbi.gov/ncic552.htm

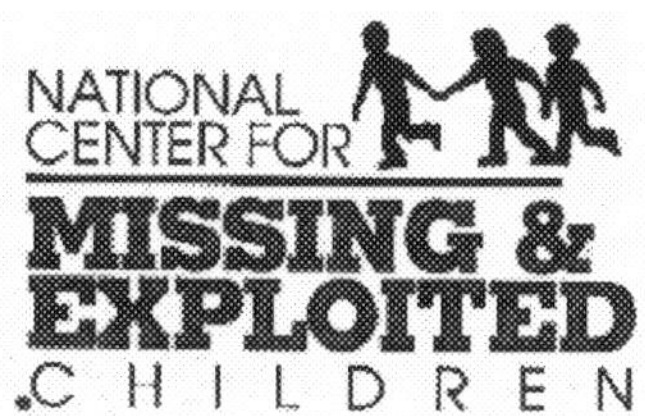

NCMEC: National Center for Missing and Exploited Children

This organization works directly with all law enforcement in cases of missing, sexually exploited, and unidentified-deceased juveniles, by offering technical assistance, resources, information dissemination, and advice, whether it be with evidence collection, preparation of search warrants, interviewing victims, conducting searches, or other aspects of investigation or prosecution.

Some of the free services NCMEC can provide include 24 hour, toll-free Hotline/CyberTipline, can provide help with cases of an international nature and provide technical-case assistance. In addition, they can help with photograph & poster preparation & rapid distribution, leads/sightings & information dissemination, age enhancement, facial reconstruction, and image/identification services. Other services include database queries, forensic services, on-site investigative assistance, abduction case training, educational materials and publications.

NDIC: National Drug Intelligence Center

NDIC is the National Drug Intelligence Center. It is under the direction of the US Attorney General's Office, Department of Justice. NDIC has been designated the nation's principal center for strategic domestic counter-drug intelligence. Some of NDIC's services include onsite searches & analysis of seized drug-related records, identification of criminal suspects & assets, linkage of suspects to other investigations, analytical support, search intelligence & open-source databases and retrieval of computerized evidence, which can be hidden, concealed, encrypted, or password protected

NDPIX: National Drug Pointer Index

NDPIX, the National Drug Pointer Index, is a fully automated pointer information system. It allows all law enforcement agencies, local, state, and federal, the ability to determine if a current drug investigative suspect is under active suspicion by another participating agency. Agencies are required to submit information to NDPIX in order to get information out of NDPIX. Information is only shared through telephone contact.

All information is stored for 180 days with the option to be renewed for another 180 days. In order to obtain information, every agency must sign a Participation Agreement with NDPIX, and have someone designated as a primary user. Each entry has 8 mandatory data elements regarding the individual entering the data, case identifier, and the target. However, each NDPIX entry may contain up to 39 data elements. The greater number of data elements entered, the greater the possibility of a match being made. All entries must be sent via NLETS & must be formatted as required. The search will only be on the data elements included in the entry.

NIBIN - National Integrated Ballistic Identification Network

The FBI (DrugFire) and the ATF (IBIS) combined their databases of ballistic information into what is now called NIBIN. NIBIN is another large database of ballistic information which compares bullet casings to unique casing identifiers which have been placed in the database. Weapons involved in drive-by shootings and other homicides have been identified using this database of information. DRUGFIRE is an automated computer technology that links firearms evidence from serial shooting investigations. As of August 18, 1997 DRUGFIRE is operational in 89 of the nearly 200 firearms laboratories in the United States. There are 99 more committed labs that will be receiving DRUGFIRE systems in the near future.

DRUGFIRE is designed to significantly increase the effectiveness of forensic laboratories in maintaining and searching Open Case Fired Ammunition Files. DRUGFIRE seamlessly integrates forensic database information, video, audio, digital images, and telecommunications technologies to simulate the functionality of forensic equipment. Through the use of state-of-the-art technologies, DRUGFIRE enhances the capabilities of the forensic firearm examiner.

The Drugfire System is used by more than 450 firearm examiners and technicians worldwide and as of October 1, 1999 there were over 225,000 images in the system which have led to over 3700 Cold Hits.

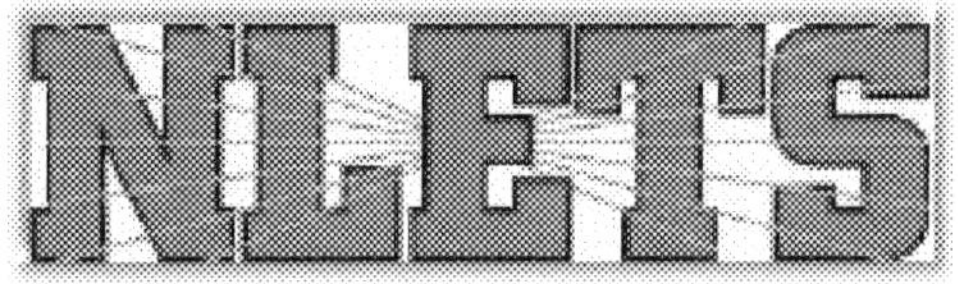

NLETS: The National Law Enforcement Telecommunications System

NLETS can be accessed through all federal, state, and local law enforcement information systems, (i.e. NCIC), or by accessing it on the world wide web at: http://www.nlets.org/

The mission of the National Law Enforcement Telecommunication System (NLETS) is to benefit, to the highest degree, the safety, security, and preservation of human life and the protection of property. NLETS will assist those governmental agencies and other organizations with similar missions who enforce or assist in enforcing local, state, or federal laws or ordinances. The National Law Enforcement Telecommunication System is a sophisticated message-switching network linking local, state, and federal agencies together to provide the capability to exchange criminal justice and public safety related information interstate.

The system is operated and controlled by the states. Every state is a member while federal systems such as the Federal Bureau of Investigation's National Crime Information Center (NCIC), U.S. Treasury's Treasury

Enforcement Communications System (TECS), Department of Justice's System (JUST), Postal Inspection Service, Naval Investigation Service, Interpol, Air Force OSI, U.S. Secret Service, Department of State, Immigration Service Law Enforcement Support Center (LESC) and other federal agencies also utilize the network.

In 1990 an interface to the Royal Canadian Mounted Police (RCMP) was established. Additionally, the National Insurance Crime Bureau (NICB) provides service to the NLETS community. New agencies continue to join at an average of about one per year.

The concept upon which NLETS is built is relatively simple. State law enforcement agencies in every state link together local agencies within their geographic boundaries by means of computers, terminals, and communication lines. NLETS links the state computers together via high-speed Frame Relay circuits. Using this concept coupled with a standardized nationwide addressing scheme, a local agency may transmit and receive from another agency outside of his or her state in a matter of seconds.

TECS: Treasury Enforcement Communications System

TECS is the Treasury Enforcement Communications System, maintained by the US Customs Service. Agencies that participate in TECS include US Customs, ATF, IRS, INTERPOL, DEA (through EPIC), and the National Credit Bureau. Access is limited to these member agencies. TECS terminals are located at all points of entry into US Territory and Customs Pre-entry Inspection points abroad.

TECS can provide information in regards to: cash transaction records (CTRs), boat registrations, in & out of country pilot records, passenger flight information (concurrent arrivals) and lookout lists for boats & aircraft traveling in & out of the United States.

ATF: Alcohol, Tobacco and Firearms

ATF retains data on distilleries, wineries, breweries, manufacturers of tobacco products, wholesale and retail dealers of alcoholic beverages, etc. They investigate reports of alleged violations and maintain data on federally licensed firearms manufacturers, importers and dealers as well as federally licensed explosive dealers, importers and manufacturers. ATF can trace firearms that have serial numbers and explosives.

 **US Department of Agriculture**

Issues surrounding meat or poultry companies, feedlot owners, livestock brokers, logging (tree harvesting) companies, import or export of agricultural commodities, animals or plants, etc.

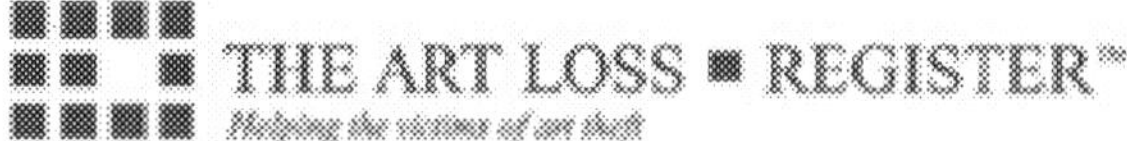 **Art Loss Register (ALR)**

A register that contains over 80,000 items of art that have been reported stolen or missing by INTERPOL, state and local police, insurance companies, the FBI, foreign governments, private collectors, art dealers and museums.

United States Department of Defense

The individual military departments do not maintain files or records pertaining to individuals no longer on active duty. When an individual is separated from military service (because of retirement, discharge from active duty, or death), his/her Field Personnel File (containing all military and health records) is forwarded for storage to the National Personnel Records Center (Military), 9700 Page Boulevard, St. Louis, Missouri 63172. The Records Center is under the jurisdiction of the National Archives and Records Administration (NARA) of the United States Government at http://www.nara.gov/regional/stlouis.html.

An individual's complete service record is available to the former service member or, if deceased, to his/her next of kin (parents, spouse, or children). Limited information (such as dates of service, awards, and training) is available to anyone. Not available to the general public is information which would invade an individual's privacy; for example, medical records, Social Security number, or present address. Go to the web link above for contact information at: http://www.defenselink.mil/faq/pis/PC03MLTR.html

Deluxe ChexSystems

Provides data on over 11 million individuals and businesses that have had their account closed for cause by their financial institution due to fraud or abuse. Reasons include automatic teller machine fraud, check kiting, and writing checks on closed accounts. Records on abused accounts are maintained for 5 years.

FBI: Federal Bureau of Investigation

The FBI can provide information on criminal records and fingerprints, as well as nonrestricted information pertaining to criminal offenses and subversive activities. It also can provide information about foreign fugitives and wanted, missing and unidentified persons.

FBI administers NCIC which maintains information of a variety of subjects such as stolen vehicles, license plates and guns. They also maintain the following indexes: State Criminal History Records, Criminal History Records of Federal Offenders, National Stolen Property Index (stolen government property) and National Fraudulent Check Index.

United States State Department

Maintains records on passports and import and export licenses. The Department's Bureau of Diplomatic Security has information on previous investigations conducted by that office.

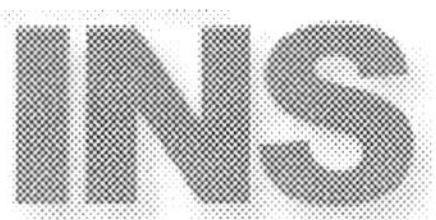

INS: Immigration and Naturalization Service

INS retains alien registration records in effect since August 1940, lists of passengers and crew on vessels from foreign ports, naturalization records, deportation proceedings and financial statements of aliens and persons sponsoring naturalized citizens.

United States Marshal's Office

USMS maintains information on individuals wanted as fugitives by the federal government and maintains records on the seizing, managing and selling of assets forfeited by drug traffickers and other criminals.

NICB: National Insurance Crime Bureau

NICB maintains an on-line computer database of 300 million records that assists law enforcement officials and insurance investigators and claims personnel in detecting fraudulent insurance claims and identifying stolen vehicles. NICB also has over 200 experienced special agents who team up with insurance investigators and law enforcement officials to uncover and prosecute vehicle theft and insurance fraud.

NWCCC: National White Collar Crime Center

The National White Collar Crime Center is dedicated to supporting law enforcement in the prevention, investigation, and prosecution of economic crimes and computer-related crimes. The Center has a database system that contains information on individuals and business suspected of economic criminal activity, including advanced fee loan schemes, credit card fraud, computer fraud and securities and investment fraud.

Department of Transportation

Records for the Federal Aviation Administration, the U.S. Coast Guard and the Federal Highway Administration. The FAA maintains records reflecting the chain of ownership of civil aircraft in the USA, including manufacturer, sale, transfers, inspections and modifications. The US Coast Guard is the primary federal agency with maritime authority in the US. The Coast Guard maintains information on U.S. Vessels, names of merchant mariners and investigative records pertaining to them, records relating to maritime drug smuggling and general criminal investigations. The Federal Highway Administration has information regarding motor carriers, licenses, inspections and registrations of interstate carriers.

RISS: Regional Information Sharing Systems

The Regional Information Sharing Systems comprise more than 4,500 local, state, and federal law enforcement agencies. Comprised of 6 regional projects, RISS operates in 50 states, the District of Columbia, and Canada. Although the projects focus on the overall objective of information sharing, each project is individualized.

The project responsible for the State of Utah is the Rocky Mountain Information Network (RMIN) which focuses on narcotics trafficking, associated criminal activity, criminal gangs, and violent crime.

Middle Atlantic-Great Lakes Organized Crime Law Enforcement Network (MAGLOCLEN) focuses on organized criminal activity, criminal gangs and violent crime.

The Mid-States Organized Crime Information Center (MOCIC) focuses on narcotics trafficking, professional traveling criminals, organized crime, criminal gangs and violent crime.

The New England State Police Information Network (NESPIN) focuses on narcotics trafficking, organized crime, major criminal activity, criminal gangs and violent crime.

The Regional Organized Crime Information Center (ROCIC) focuses on narcotics violators, professional traveling criminals, organized crime, criminal gangs and violent crime.

The final project, the Western States Information Network (WISN) concentrates on narcotics and trafficking and criminal organizations and associations.

United States Secret Service

The Secret Service is responsible for investigating the counterfeiting of currency and securities; forgery and altering of government checks and bonds; thefts and fraud relating to Treasury electronic funds transfers; financial access, telecommunications, computer, and telemarketing fraud; fraud concerning federally insured financial institutions; and other criminal and non-criminal cases.

The Forensic Services Division also operated a hybrid Automated Fingerprint Identification System, the largest of its kind with more than 25 million fingerprints. Other services are polygraph consultation or assistance, photographic, graphic, age progression/regression; and voice and image enhancement technology.

SPICIN: South Pacific Islands Criminal Intelligence Network

In the South Pacific, (SPICIN) the South Pacific Islands Criminal Intelligence Network comprises 21 countries. The purpose of SPICIN is to promote the gathering, recording and exchanging of information not otherwise available through normal channels. Information is available on drug trafficking, mobile criminals, organized crime, terrorism and the use of the Pacific Island waters and aircraft, and other information of a criminal nature.

United States Postal Inspector's Office

As one of our country's oldest federal law enforcement agencies, founded by Benjamin Franklin, the United States Postal Inspection Service has a long, proud and successful history of fighting criminals who attack our nation's postal system and misuse it to defraud, endanger or otherwise threaten the American public. As the primary law enforcement arm of the United States Postal Service, the U.S. Postal Inspection Service is a highly specialized, professional organization performing investigative and security functions essential to a stable and sound postal system.

As fact-finding and investigative agents, Postal Inspectors are federal law enforcement officers who carry firearms, make arrests and serve federal search warrants and subpoenas. Inspectors work closely with U.S. Attorneys, other law enforcement agencies and local prosecutors to investigate postal cases and prepare them for court. There are approximately 2,000 Postal Inspectors stationed throughout the United States who enforce over 200 federal laws covering investigations of crimes that adversely affect or fraudulently use the U.S. Mail and postal system.

To assist in carrying out its responsibilities, the Postal Inspection Service maintains a Security Force staffed by 1,400 uniformed Postal Police Officers who are assigned to critical postal facilities throughout the country. The officers provide perimeter security, escort high-value mail shipments and perform other essential protective functions.

The Postal Inspection Service operates five forensic crime laboratories, strategically located in cities across the country. The labs are staffed with forensic scientists and technical specialists, who assist Inspectors in analyzing evidentiary material needed for identifying and tracing criminal suspects and in providing expert testimony for cases brought to trial.

CALEA Implementation Section
Communications Assistance For Law Enforcement Act

In 1994, the 103rd Congress passed the CALEA (Communications Assistance for Law Enforcement Act) to ensure that as technology changes, that law enforcement is able to conduct lawfully authorized intercepts. The FBI's CALEA Implementation Section oversees this mission and is composed of four units representing law enforcement and includes a state and local forum that meets regularly.

Section 103 of CALEA sets forth the assistance capability requirements that telecommunications carriers need to maintain to support law enforcement in the conduct of lawfully-authorized electronic surveillance. Pursuant to a court order or other lawful authorization, carriers must be able to: (1) expeditiously isolate all wire and electronic communications of a target transmitted by the carrier within its service area; (2) expeditiously isolate call-identifying information of a target; (3) provide intercepted communications and call-identifying information to law enforcement; and (4) carry out intercepts unobtrusively, so targets are not made aware of the electronic surveillance, and in a manner that does not compromise the privacy and security of other communications.

Abbreviations

AFIS	Automated Fingerprint Identification System
ALR	Art Loss Register
ATF	Bureau of Alcohol, Tobacco and Firearms
CALEA	Communications Assistance for Law Enforcement Act
CFTC	Commodity Futures Trading Commission
CIS	Central Index System
CLASS	Consular Lookout and Support System
CODIS	Combined DNA Index System
DCII	Defense Central and Investigations Index
DEA	Drug Enforcement Administration
DECA	Development of Espionage Counterintelligence and Counter-terrorism Awareness
DLR	Division of Labor Racketeering
DOD	Department of Defense
DOJ	Department of Justice
EDGAR	Electronic Data Gathering and Retrieval
e-mail	electronic mail
EPIC	El Paso Intelligence Center
FAA	Federal Aviation Administration
FBI	Federal Bureau of Investigation
FCC	Federal Communications Commission
FDA	Food and Drug Administration
FDIC	Federal Deposit Insurance Corporation
FERC	Federal Energy Regulatory Commission
FHWA	Federal Highway Administration
FinCEN	Financial Crimes Enforcement Network
FIRS	Fingerprint Identification Records System
FTP	File Transfer Protocol
FTRACK	Felony Tracking (Utah Department of Corrections)
GILS	Government Information Locator System
HHS	Department of Health and Human Services
IAFIS	Integrated Automated Fingerprint Idetification System
IBIS	Interagency Border Inspection System
ICTS	International Criminal Police Organization Case-Tracking System
IFAR	International Foundation for Art Research
III	Interstate Identification Index
INS	Immigration and Naturalization Service
INTERPOL	International Criminal Police Organization
IRC	Internet Relay Chat
IRS	Internal Revenue Service

JMIE   Joint Maritime Information Element
LEIU   Law Enforcement Intelligence Unit
LESC   Law Enforcement Support Center
MAGLOCLEN   Middle Atlantic-Great Lakes Organized Crime Law
            Enforcement Network
MOCIC   Mid-States Organized Crime Information Center
NADDIS   Narcotics and Dangerous Drugs Information System
NAIL   NARA Archival Information Locator
NAILS   National Alien Information Lookout System
NARA   National Archives and Records Administration
NASA   National Aeronautics and Space Administration
NCIC   National Crime Information Center
NCMEC   National Center for Missing and Exploited Children
NCUA   National Credit Union Administration
NDIC   National Drug Intelligence Center
NDPIX   National Drug Pointer Index
NESPIN   New England State Police Information Network
NFIC   National Fraud Information Center
NIBIN   National Integrated Ballistic Identification Network
NICB   National Insurance Crime Bureau
NIIS   Nonimmigrant Information System
NLETS   National Law Enf.Telecommunications System
NRC   Nuclear Regulatory Commission
NTC   National Tracing Center
OSI   Office of Special Investigations
RISS   Regional Information Sharing System
RMIN   Rocky Mountain Information Network
ROCIC   Regional Organized Crime Information Center
SBA   Small Business Administration
SEC   Securities and Exchange Commission
SPICIN   South Pacific Islands Criminal Intelligence Network
SSA   Social Security Administration
TECS   Treasury Enforcement Communications System
USDA   U.S. Department of Agriculture
USMS   U.S. Marshals Service
USNCB   U.S. National Central Bureau
VA   Department of Veterans Affairs
WAIS   Wide Area Information Server
WHD   Wage Hour Division
WSIN   Western States Information Network
WWW   World Wide Web

REFERENCES:

Most of the references for this chapter are taken from the world wide web for each individual organization.

(April 1997 United States General Accounting Office "Investigators Guide to Sources of Information" Washington DC, GAO/OSI-92-2)

IAFIS, http://www.fbi.gov/hq/cjisd/iafis.htm), 2001

CODIS, http://www.fbi.gov/hq/lab/codis/index1.htm), 2001

DRUGFIRE, http://www.fbi.gov, 2001

What is the average number of missing persons (nationally)?

103,040

What is the average number of unidentified bodies (nationally)?

3,900

In 1960, what was the solution rate in percentages for homicide?

90%

In 1990, what was the solution rate in percentages for homicide?

70%

Name two programs that are providing Criminal Investigative Analysis
assistance in the United States today.

VICAP   VTAP

- chapter three-

EXPANDING TRADITIONS IN LAW ENFORCEMENT

Abstract

Law enforcement faces many challenges as it fulfills its mission of protecting life and property. A critical shortcoming in the law enforcement profession is the lack of cooperation, communication and coordination. This problem is compounded when personalities, perceived power, politics, funding or lack of experience are mixed into the investigation of crime and criminal behavior. There are thousands of law enforcement agencies and hundreds of thousands of sworn peace officers in the United States of America, each working within its own jurisdictional boundaries and often protecting its own "turf." This paper will evaluate the problem of serial offenders and the impact law enforcement can have on this type of offender if they can correct this failure to communicate and cooperate in the solving of difficult criminal cases.

In view of the many challenges in the field of public safety today, law enforcement professionals must be willing to consider any legitimate investigative approach to enhance the probability of success in solving crimes. This may require a shift from one of personal experience and an open look ahead to unfamiliar territory. Every great discovery requires the exploration of uncharted terrain, leading law enforcement to new maps and ways of thinking while creating quantum leaps of advancement in every field of knowledge. Through these challenges, today's enforcers become better investigators and public servants. Often, it is easy to become so entrenched in the "way it's always been done," that it becomes difficult to envision new concepts and approaches.

In his intuitive comments entitled "Pulling Rank" in the magazine of the Naval Institute, <u>Proceedings</u>, Frank Koch shared his paradigm-shifting experience and realization that authority does not always mean correctness (1987).

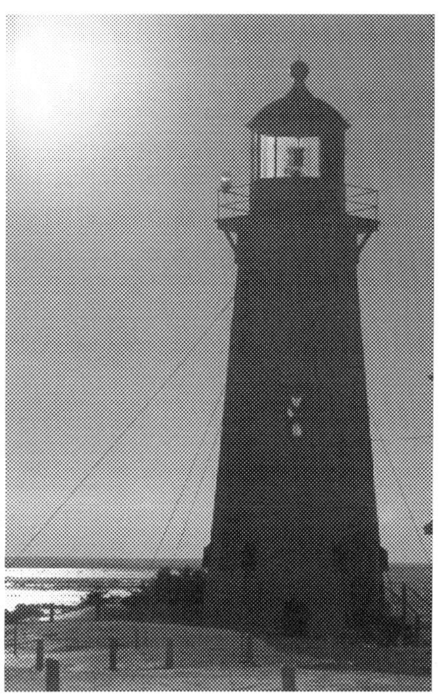

Paradigm-Shifting Experience

Two battleships assigned to the training squadron had been at sea on maneuvers in heavy weather for several days. I was serving on the lead battleship and was on the bridge as night fell. The visibility was poor with patchy fog, so the captain remained on the bridge keeping an eye on all activities. Shortly after dark, the lookout on the wing of the bridge reported, "Light, bearing on the starboard bow."

"Is it steady or moving astern?" the Captain called out. The lookout replied, "Steady, Captain," which meant we were in a dangerous collision course with that ship. The Captain then called to the signalman, "Signal that ship: We are on a collision course. Advise you change course 20 degrees." Back came the message, "I suggest you make a course change of 20 degrees." The captain said, "Send: "I am a Captain. Change course 20 degrees."

"I am a seaman second-class," came the reply. "Again, advise you change course 20 degrees." By that time the Captain was furious. He spat out, "Send: I am a battleship, change course 20 degrees." Back came the flashing light, "I'm a lighthouse. Your call."

Immediately, we changed course. (p. 81)

Over and over, law enforcement agencies complain of information droughts that not only extend from agency to agency, but often within single departments. More frustrating is the complaint that when discussing the lack of information sharing with administrations, too often the supervisor's justification is centered more around their "perceived authority" than common sense.

According to the 1997 report by the United States Department of Justice on <u>Law Enforcement Management and Administrative Statistics</u> (1999), there are 18,769 law enforcement agencies in the country. Within those agencies there are over 663,500 sworn peace officers (p. xi). The number of peace officers in the United States, and the diverse makeup of the agencies they work for result in many different approaches to handling crime. Each policing organization has independent programs and missions, based on the community served and the crime problems addressed. Yet as different as each agency is, they all have the same basic responsibilities in dealing with crime, criminals and criminal behavior.

Without an expansive communication network and cohesive program of sharing information, the challenges of linking crimes and criminals together is nearly impossible. Since the inception of <u>UTAP</u>, the <u>U</u>tah <u>c</u>riminal <u>T</u>racking and <u>A</u>nalysis <u>P</u>roject (UTAP, 1997), investigators have had the opportunity to interview dozens of serial offenders ranging from child abusers, rapists, white-collar predators and murderers. In those interviews, prisoners in Utah and other United States prisons commented on their basic technique in avoiding law enforcement detection. The common theme is that they move from one location to another before the police figure out who they are. They operate under the practice explained by a Utah State Correctional Inmate B.N. who

"What we've got here is failure to communicate. Some men you just can't reach. I don't like it any more than you"

Cool Hand Luke, 1967
Warner Brothers
Productions

stated, "if they [law enforcement] ever do figure it out, you're long gone" (Inmate B.N., 2001).

Criminals plan on law enforcement's lack of communication, cooperation and coordination to find success in their efforts to victimize others. It is not uncommon for a criminal to burglarize a home in Salt Lake City, Utah, and within hours drive to an adjacent community such as Ogden, Utah, to pawn or "fence" the stolen property. By simply moving from one law enforcement jurisdiction to another, the property thief improves his chances of avoiding detection and ultimate apprehension. If the item stolen is pawned, it may be months or years before investigators manually sort through the thousands of pawn tickets generated each year, in hopes of identifying the stolen property or weapon obtained, or used in the commission of a crime.

In the motion picture <u>Cool Hand Luke</u> (1967), the captain of a Georgia prison is speaking to the recaptured prisoner, Luke (Paul Newman), and says, "What we've got here is failure to communicate. Some men you just can't reach... I don't like it any more than you" (Pearce/Warner Brothers). This classic statement from film clearly represents the problem faced by today's law officers. We are tragically suffering from a "failure to communicate." We are not effectively communicating within individual law enforcement agencies as well as with outside agencies.

In January of 2001, a newly assigned detective (WS Investigator, 2001) from a western (to remain nameless) state who was working on a "cold case" homicide, told of this experience he had with officers from his own department who failed to share information during an investigation.

Shortly after becoming a new detective, I found myself sitting all alone at my desk at the conclusion of my shift. I sat in my chair, with my feet up, looking around and thinking about how "cool" it was to have finally made it into the investigations division.

As I reflected on my great fortune, my attention was drawn to a ceiling tile above my desk that was shifted - slightly out of place. I stared at the tile for a moment, and then dismissed it, leaving for the night. That evening, my thoughts returned again and again to that "crazy ceiling tile." The next day I busied myself with my investigative duties and went home without thinking about the tile again. Later that night, as I thought of my caseload and my duties, I reflected again on the tile. Those thoughts eventually piquedmy curiosity and I vowed to check the tile the next morning. Early the following morning, I climbed onto my desk, moved back the tile and noticed about 3 inches of stacked papers. The papers turned out to be a case report from a homicide that had occurred 11 years earlier. Closer inspection of the case report revealed that the investigator who hid the report had information that could solve the case.

As I studied and learned more about the case, I discovered that several investigators from my agency and another "outside" agency were competitively investigating the case and trying to be the "one" investigator or agency to solve the murder. To each of them, being the "hero" was more important than successfully bringing the case to conclusion. Unfortunately, the case information cooled and a short

The Three C's
- ***Communication***
- ***Cooperation***
- ***Coordination***

time later the investigator died. The information went unseen for eleven years until discovered in the ceiling.

In reading the report, the investigator identified the name of the witness, along with all of the pertinent contact information, including the name of the suspect who committed the murder and the burial site of the victim. The investigator enthusiastically searched for the witness, only to learn that this most valuable witness had died one week before the investigator's discovery of the case report. To this day, the investigator is confident that he knows who murdered the victim, but he cannot completely tie the case together in a manner that could warrant homicide charges. The investigator's commentary helped fuel the need for this paper and the focus on cooperation, communication and coordination. Quoting the investigator, "If they [the agencies and investigators] had only worked closer together instead of each trying to be the hero, the offender might be in prison today" (2001).

In addition to the problems surrounding the three C's (communication, cooperation and coordination), law enforcement also experiences other challenges. Reports of investigations being hampered because of politics, agency makeup or lack of resources are far too common and completely inappropriate. An investigation may be concluded prematurely or not investigated at all if it doesn't fit the political climate of the community. Another case may be closed based on funding or because of a low level of experience in dealing with complex crimes such as white-collar investigations. Lack of training or experiential inability to evaluate and recognize difficult crimes, such as electronic theft or internet crime, joins the list.

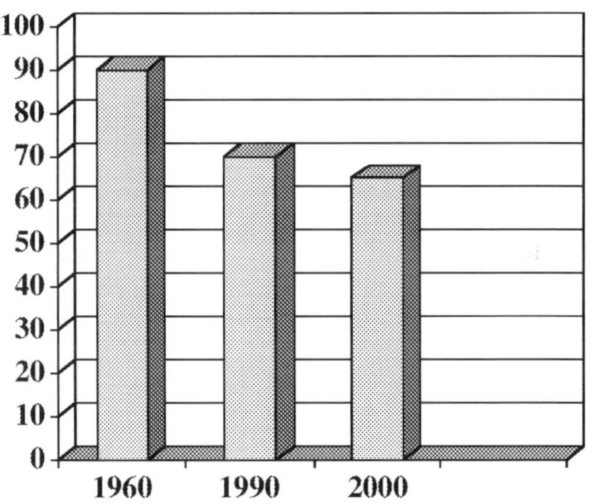

With this list of possibilities, we must also consider that today's criminals are much more mobile than they have been in the past. For law enforcement agencies to keep the information gained about criminals or criminal enterprises operating in their community to themselves should be unethical and/or criminal, in and of itself.

Decades ago, a traveling salesperson might be on the road for weeks as he traveled from community to community or from his hometown to the city in which he worked. Today, that same salesperson could be working in New York City in the morning, and relaxing on the West Coast in time for dinner. Or, rather than making a sales call, the criminal could be in California committing a sexual assault in the morning, and later that evening be thousands of miles away from the crime scene, the police and the investigation.

In the 1960's American law officers were solving ninety percent of all crimes of homicide. Today, they are solving approximately sixty-nine percent (Department of Justice Statistics 1960-1999).

In a condemning article in <u>USA Today</u> (2000) titled, "More Homicides Are Going Unsolved," we learn that our solved murder rate numbers may actually be dropping further (p.1). Based on that article and discussions with homicide investigators across the country, it is estimated that nearly 35 to 40

percent of all homicides in the United States are going unsolved (King, 1997-2001).

There are many reasons for the changes we are experiencing in the rate of solving crimes. Some people theorize that today's criminals are becoming more sophisticated. For instance, criminal offenders have adapted and improved their ability to avoid detection by more frequently wearing gloves or different kinds of shoes. The criminal expects investigators to look for forensic evidence like fingerprints, shoeprints, etc. If we are to accept the premise that the criminal is adapting and improving, then shouldn't it be true that current day enforcers have improved their investigative ability, efforts and response to criminal activity?

Some argue that today's citizens are less involved in their communities and less apt to know who their neighbors are in comparison to 40 years ago. As people move around in this more transient lifestyle, they are less intimately involved in the communities they live in. In fact, some people move so often that they may be less inclined to develop relationships in their neighborhoods at all.

Robert Ben Rhoades, 2001

We should closely examine and consider the possibility presented earlier of a more mobile offender who is traveling throughout any given state, region or country as a part of a daily routine. Let's examine the case of Robert Ben Rhoades, (a serial sex abuser and murderer). Rhoades, who is serving a life sentence for homicide at Joliet Correctional Facility in Joliet,

Illinois (Illinois Appellate Brief, 2001), is considered one of the most dangerous and notorious serial killers in the United States. Some investigators suggest that he is responsible for killing as many as fifty to three hundred people but has only been convicted of one homicide for which he is incarcerated. Other charges could be filed if Rhoades ever manages to get an early released from his life sentence in Illinois.

Robert Ben Rhoades is the perfect example of a serial killer who is also the most vicious of serial sexual predators... the "Anger Retaliatory" rapist, or "Devil" rapist as described in the landmark rapist typology profiling forms developed by Gregory M. Cooper (Cooper, 1999).

Peterbuilt truck driven by Robert Ben Rhoades at time of arrest.

Rhoades was a professional long-haul truck driver and his case dramatically demonstrates the sophistication of a criminal predator who effectively defies law enforcement resources due to fragmented efforts and inconsistent investigative approaches.

On April 1, 1990, Trooper Mike Miller, an Arizona highway patrolman, observed a semi-tractor-trailer parked on the shoulder of I-10. The trooper stopped to offer assistance and made a discovery that would impact states across America, from the East to West Coasts. As Miller approached and looked inside the running 18-wheeler, he observed a bound, nude, white female in the sleeper berth of the cab. A horse-type bit and bridle was in the mouth of the terrified victim who was chained to the interior of the truck.

Also in the sleeper berth was Robert Ben Rhoades, who, when surprised by the trooper's advance, immediately exited the truck, trying to convince Trooper Miller that nothing was wrong. Rhoades stated that the events being discovered were consensual and a private matter.

While Trooper Miller tried to sort through the situation, he placed

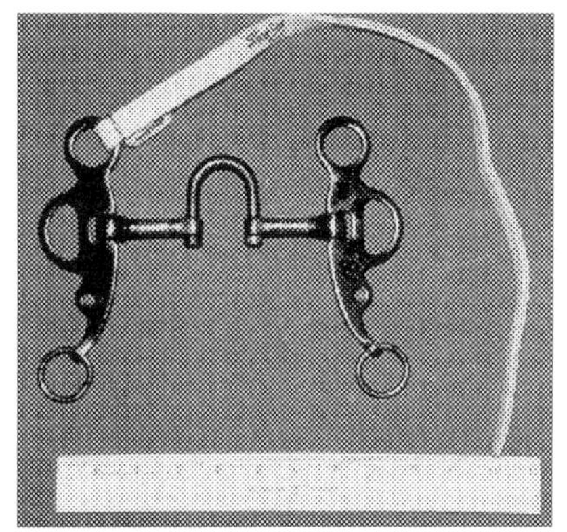

Rhoades under arrest, at which time he discovered Rhoades to be in possession of a loaded .25 Caliber automatic pistol (Brandel, 1996, p.1). Rhoades was placed into the troopers vehicle and secured with a seatbelt. By the time Trooper Miller checked on the victim and returned to the squad car, Rhoades had managed to get the seatbelt off and slip his handcuffed hands in front of him. Miller, reflecting on the handcuffs and restraints on the victim, asked Rhoades if he had a handcuff key to which Rhoades affirmatively replied. Trooper Miller took the key, re-cuffed Rhoades behind his back and through his belt and stayed with him until backup officers arrived at the scene to assist him.

After the terrified victim (who was later identified as Lisa Pennal) was released, she recounted her story of abduction and torture. She stated that she had accepted a ride with Rhoades at a coffee shop in Buckeye, Arizona. Although Pennal was difficult to interview and spoke in fractured sentences, the investigators learned of her transient lifestyle and current drug abuse. Pennal stated that she was carrying secret information to Washington D.C., and that the CIA was after her and that they, and Rhoades, wanted to kill her. The investigator noted that she was dressed in a skirt and shirt, but that she was only wearing slippers on her feet that were designed like a cartoon tiger.

The victim indicated that she fell asleep in the sleeper berth, only to awake as Rhoades was placing handcuffs on her wrists and ankles. She stated that Rhoades beat her with a whip, attached a chain around her neck, and attached spring-type clips to her nipples and vagina. It was unclear how long Rhoades kept Lisa Pennal in this torture chamber, but the physical injuries on her body indicated that several events of whipping and torture had occurred. During this ordeal, Rhoades told Pennal that he had been doing this type of thing for 15 years.

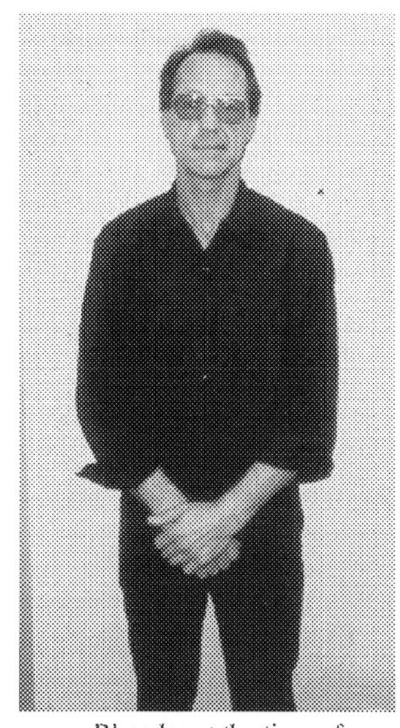

Rhoades at the time of questioning on the victim from Buckeye, Arizona

The investigators in this case faced a difficult situation because Rhoades was so convincing. Even though he was handcuffed and in custody, he remained very calm. He made light of the mental capacity of the victim and tried to get the investigator to sympathize with him as he described her as the aggressor in the event, referring to her as a "lot lizard." In the book, "Roadside Prey" by Alva Busch, Rhoades is quoted as saying, "I can tell you, this girl is not playing with a full deck," laughed Rhoades, as if someone had told a joke... "She ain't wrapped too tight," chuckled Rhoades, "you don't screw around with the women on the road. Not unless you want your dick to drop off, okay?"... "She wanted to go to bed."... "I was dragging anchor. She was going back to bed. I said, 'Go ahead." She started taking off her clothes, and I said "What the #$*^#' And I let her" (1996, pg. 58-62).

The victim, who was hysterical at times, showed evidence of sustained physical and sexual abuse, corroborating her story of captivation. Rhoades' explanation began to fall apart as investigators discovered large amounts of bondage type pornography and sexual assault materials in his truck. What

Rhoades was verbalizing was not being supported by the non-verbal clues that the investigators were uncovering.

During the subsequent investigation, search warrants were executed on the cab of the semi-tractor truck and on Robert Ben Rhoades' residence in Houston, Texas. The results of the searches revealed a briefcase containing whips, handcuffs, spring-type clips, a dildo, various items of women's clothing, miscellaneous paperwork, and several photographs of a young white female in various poses, both nude and partially dressed.

There were Polaroid® photographs of several women inside "open-roofed" vehicles, apparently taken from inside the trucker's cab as the women passed him on the highway. These photographs were seized from Rhoades' Houston apartment. There were also photographs of one particular victim (a teenage girl) in the sleeper berth of the trucker's cab, in the outdoors, and in an abandoned barn-type structure. In this particular set of photographs, the victim was handcuffed, chained, posing with a dildo, and had spring-type clips attached to her nipples.

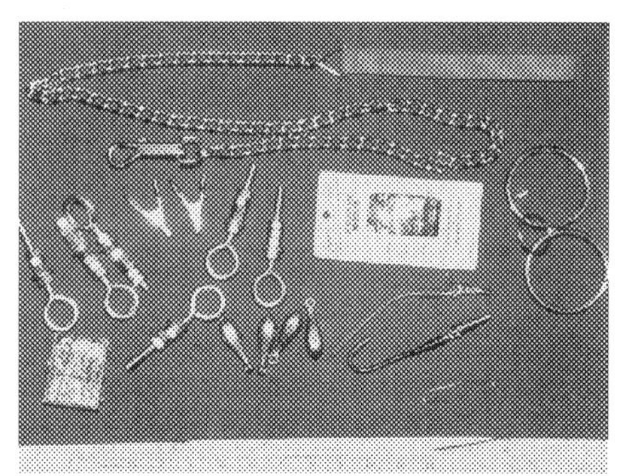

The teenager in the photographs remained unidentified as far as the Robert Ben Rhoades case was concerned. One September 29, 1990, the decomposed body of a young female was found in an abandoned barn near

Greenville, Illinois. The cause of death was determined to be ligature strangulation. The victim was later identified as 14-year-old Regina Walters. Walters was a reported runaway from Pasadena, Texas, nearly eight months before her remains were discovered in the abandoned barn. At the time of the initial missing persons report, Walters was in the company of an 18-year-old white male named Ricky Lee Jones. The two were reportedly hitchhiking to New Mexico. Ricky Lee Jones has not been located as of this writing.

Interestingly, the investigators working the Rhoades case, and the investigators working the Walters case in Texas and Illinois were each working independent of one another. Finally, through teletype and national databases, they started working together. In March of 1991, the Illinois State Police received this letter from Regina Walters' mother.

Dear Sir:

In September 1990, the police in Illinois found the remains of Regina Kay Walters. She disappeared February 3, 1990, from Pasadena, Texas. She was only fourteen years old at the time, and my only daughter. At this time the police have not brought to justice the person who has done this to my child. Even though we did not live in Illinois, this case should still be kept open. No child's death should be given up. It could happen again.

At that time, the police in Illinois asked us to keep this out of the media. We have done that and more. Just because you haven't heard from us doesn't mean we don't care. We were trying to give you time to find Regina's killer. Please don't give up. What if it was one of your children? You couldn't rest, knowing there is someone out there who took someone you loved, and don't ever think we didn't love Regina, because she was very much loved. So please don't quit looking for the killer of Regina Kay Walters.

Sincerely,
Carolyn S. Walters
(Roadside Prey, 1996, pg. 137-138).

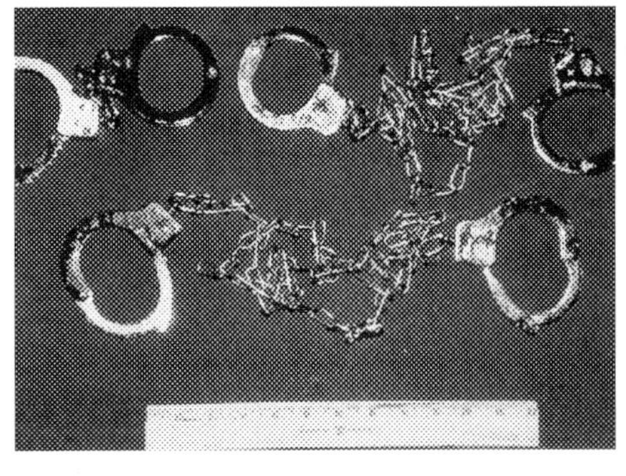

Tragically, Robert Ben Rhoades would remain a "single episode" until September 28, 1991 when he would be tied to the death of Regina Kay Walters. There are no photos of Ricky Lee Jones in Rhoades collection, but there was a journal entry in a small notebook found in Rhoades possession at the time of his arrest that states, "Ricky is a dead man" (Evidence, 1990). Police also recovered several items of clothing that belonged to Walters in the possession of Robert Ben Rhoades (1990).

Reflecting on comment Rhoades made, that he had been "doing this for 15 years," investigators looked more closely into his trucking records. They discovered that the murderous trucker had traveled extensively from the shores of the Pacific Ocean to the East Coast of New Jersey. He specifically traveled through Washington, Oregon, California, Arizona, Utah, New

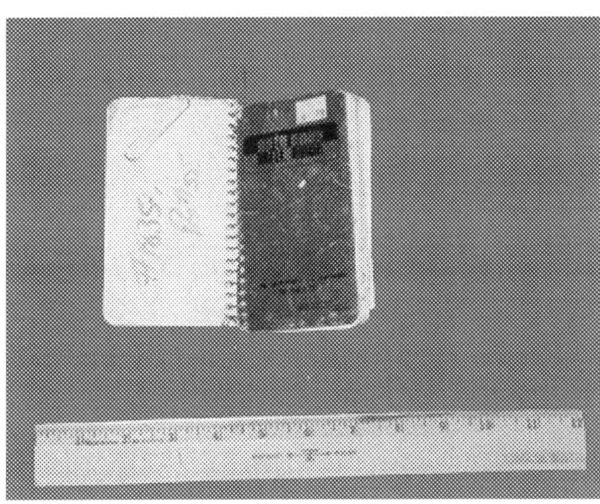

Mexico, Texas, Arkansas, Louisiana, Oklahoma, Mississippi, Florida, Georgia, Missouri, Tennessee, Illinois, Kentucky, Indiana, Ohio, Virginia, Pennsylvania and New Jersey (1990).

Suddenly, the many missing persons, unidentified bodies and unsolved homicide cases in each of those states took on new meaning. Law enforcement agencies began to share information about similar crimes and victims more generously than at any time before this incident. Since the Rhoades case broke, there have been many missing persons and unsolved homicide cases that have been attributed to Rhoades, but he has only been prosecuted on the death of Regina Walters.

This "single episode," while not forgotten, joined the huge caseload of Detective Susan Trammell, receiving less investigative attention as leads cooled and time passed. During this same period of time, Rhoades continued to travel from one state to another. As the Rhoades saga progressed, information about another victim named Shana Holts, from January of 1990, came in to contact with Rhoades at a truck stop in San Bernardino, California.

Shana Holts escaped Rhoades' torture and reported the terrifying incident, mirroring the events that Trooper Miller uncovered. Holts was so terrified of Rhoades, that when she was faced with the prospect of identifying him after fleeing his vehicle, and then of having to testify against him, she declined to cooperate any further and the case was dismissed.

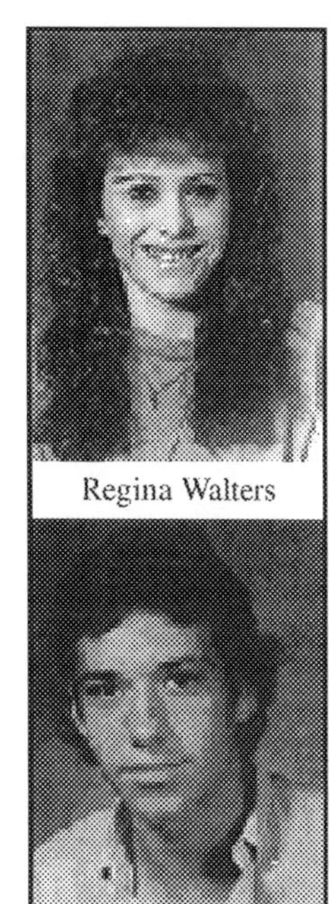
Regina Walters

Ricky Lee Jones

Rhoades at time of
booking

Other similar situations were discovered as time went on. Law enforcement agencies in many different parts of the United States had criminal abductions and possible homicide charges against Rhoades based on comparisons and travel routes. In each of those incidents, the individual agencies initially believed they were dealing with a single event, pertaining only to their jurisdiction. It wasn't until the final chapter of the Rhoades saga was written, that the agencies came to realize that their "single event" was the work of a sadistic, serial rapist and murderer.

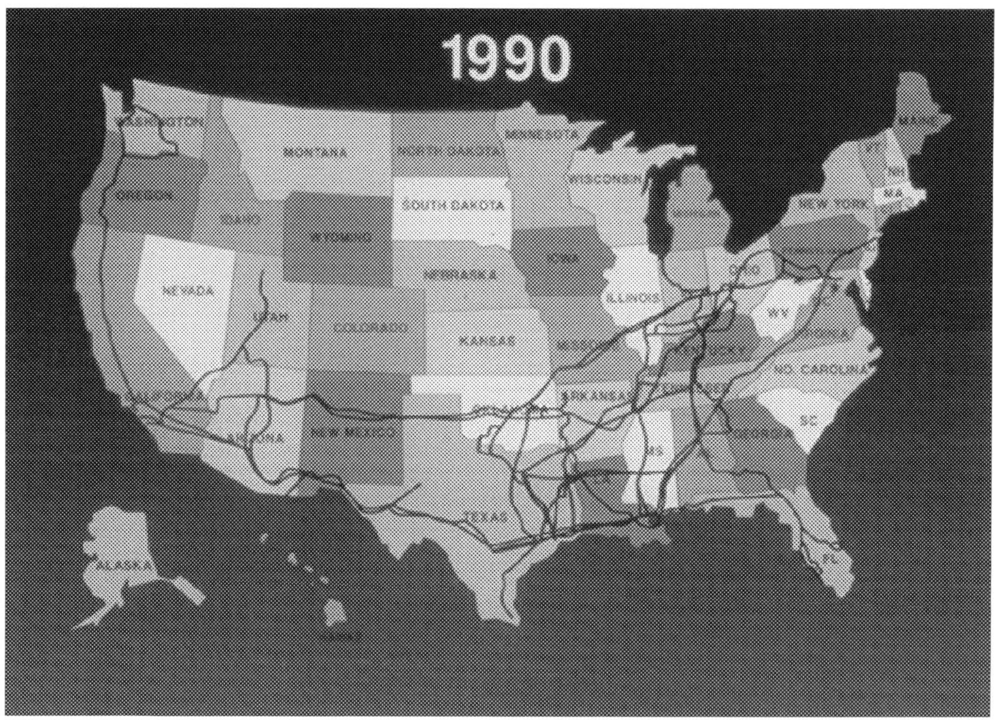

The Rhoades case has helped law enforcement agencies across the United States to see, in graphic detail, the value of cooperating, communicating and coordinating their efforts in solving difficult criminal cases. If better information sharing and coordination had occurred, it might have dramatically reduced the number of victims who fell prey to Robert Ben Rhoades.

On September 11, 1992, Robert Ben Rhoades (defendant), pursuant to negotiations with the State of Illinois, pled guilty to first-degree murder and was sentenced to imprisonment for natural life. The sentence of death had been a possibility because on May 6, 1992, the State had filed a notice that it intended to seek the death penalty. He currently resides in the Joliet Correctional Facility in Joliet, Illinois (Illinois, 2001).

With the Rhoades case in mind, let's sum up what this issue is about. When Regina Walters left Pasadena, Texas with Ricky Lee Jones, the case was handled as a single episode, runaway teen. ATL's (Attempt to Locate) were broadcast, but the extended reach of those broadcasts is unknown. Initially, a FBI ViCAP Missing Person's report was not filed. The ViCAP form (<u>Vi</u>olent <u>c</u>riminal <u>A</u>pprehension <u>P</u>rogram) is a product of the FBI's National Center for the Analysis of Violent Crime (ViCAP, 2001). The ViCAP program offers comprehensive evaluation and comparison in cases of Unsolved Homicides, Missing Persons (where foul play is suspected) and Unidentified Bodies.

National databases like the FBI's ViCAP program (ViCAP, 1984-2001), the UTAP Project (UTAP, 1997), and other local and regional investigators meetings can bridge the gap that currently exists in this regard. Through innovative policing, more can be done to help reduce crime and victimization in America.

In conclusion, if American law enforcers could foster a stronger commitment toward cooperation, communication and coordination, we would see a dramatic decrease in the time it takes to successfully resolve difficult criminal cases. By working in a cooperative manner, regardless of politics, funding or other "pet" considerations, investigators could more appropriately concentrate on solving crimes in a timely and efficient manner. Multi-agency investigators meetings and joint task force approaches, as well as sufficient training and experience will equate to increased success in the responsibility to identify, track and apprehend criminal offenders.

References

Brandel, K. (1996, February 29). Dead end, sexual sadist and cold-blooded killer Robert Ben Rhoades was a travelin' man until..., <u>Tucson Weekly</u>, p. 1.

Bush, Alva (1996). <u>Roadside Prey</u>. New York: Kensington Publishing.

Cooper, G. (1999). <u>Profiling rapists and rape typologies</u>. Provo, Utah.

Department of Justice (1960-1999). <u>Bureau of Justice Statistics.</u> D.C.

Department of Justice (1999). <u>1997 LEMAS Report.</u> Washington D.C.

Evidence (1990). <u>State of Arizona vs. Robert Ben Rhoades.</u> Arizona.

Illinois Appellate Court (July 13, 2001). <u>People v. Rhoades Case No. 5-98-0821.</u> Illinois.

Inmate B.N. (2001, July). Personal Interview. Utah State Prison.

King, M (1997-2001). <u>Personal Interviews and UTAP/ViCAP Directorship</u>. USA/Utah.

Koch, F. (November 1987). Pulling Rank <u>Proceedings</u>, Annapolis MD: US Naval Institute p. 81.

Pearce, D. (1999). <u>Cool Hand Luke</u>. New York: Avalon Press.

USA Today (February 22, 2000). <u>More Homicides Are Going Unsolved</u>. Arlington VA.

UTAP (1997-2001). <u>Organizational structure</u>. Salt Lake City, Utah.

ViCAP (1984-2001). <u>Organizational structure and development of the Violent criminal Apprehension Program submission forms</u>. Federal Bureau of Investigations, Quantico, VA.

Warner Brothers Productions & Stuart Rosenberg (Director) (1967). <u>Cool Hand Luke</u>, [Film] California.

WS Investigator (2001, January). <u>Personal Interview</u>, USA.

Chapter Review

When considering the challenges faced by today's law enforcers, what are the Three C's?

1. _______________________________   2. _______________________________

3. _______________________________

What are some additional challenges that today's enforcers face:

1. _______________________________   2. _______________________________

3. _______________________________   4. _______________________________

What are the statistical chances of solving homicides in the United States in:

1960? _______________________________   1990? _______________________________

2000? _______________________________

and what are some reasons to explain the numbers and trends exhibited?

____

____

____

____

What are some of the current databases and strategies in use to assist law enforcement in working together more effectively?

____

____

____

Notes

- chapter four-

FORMS OF EVIDENCE AND THE INTRODUCTION OF BEHAVIOR AS THE NEW FORM OF EVIDENCE

Abstract

Traditionally, courtrooms in America have become accustom to admitting into trial and accepting value in four traditional forms of evidence. Prosecutors and defense attorneys alike develop their judicial strategies and questions around physical or forensic evidence, circumstantial evidence, eyewitness accounts and participant confessions. Because of the importance of truth in these settings, the criminal justice system must demand that proper care and introduction of evidence be of a paramount concern. This paper will explore each of these forms briefly, and then introduce a "new" form of evidence... behavior, and the benefit it can have in developing motive, prosecutorial theme and even providing assistance in areas such as jury member selection.

There are four traditional forms of evidence that law enforcement officers and criminal prosecutors deal with, in part or whole, on every criminal case they handle. How the court deals with this evidence impacts the type and length of sentence (if any) that the defendant receives. Once a sentence is handed down by the court, the correctional system is required to deliver the punishment and rehabilitation opportunity for the convicted offender in a manner that is efficient and appropriate.

These traditional forms of evidence may be clearly manifested, or they may take closer observation to detect, but they are there. The four types of evidence are; physical or forensic, circumstantial, eyewitness accounts and participant confessions. In American courtrooms, these forms of evidence are

"A man's behavior is the index of the man, and his discourse is the index of his understanding."

Ali ibn-Abi-Talib

Sentences (7th century), Translated by Simon Oakley

introduced in every civil and criminal case that is heard by a judge or magistrate.

Chief Justice Marshall, in the case of Marbury v. Madison stated, "The very essence of civil liberty certainly consists in the right of every individual to claim the protection of the laws, whenever he receives an injury. One of the first duties of the government is to afford that protection. The government of the United States has been emphatically termed a government of laws, and not of men. It will certainly cease to deserve this high appellation, if the law furnish no remedy for the violation of a vested legal right" (Marbury v. Madison, 1803). What Justice Marshall was saying is that fashioning remedies to insure against governmental abuse cannot be left to the brutal clash of political powers or by deference to any "elite" group of men. The secret to preserving a free society is found in implementing a belief that all people, including those who enforce the law are accountable to an orderly system that is ultimately responsible to the people (Utah Prosecutor Handbook, 2000, p. 27).

In order for the prosecution, the courts and corrections to function properly, each must rely on the authority and limitations of law enforcement's power and responsibility to act justly in the investigation and presentation of all criminal cases. Consider the four traditional types of evidence used in the State of Utah v. Ronald and Daniel Lafferty homicide case, including the way in which the "new" form of evidence (behavior) clarified some issues and made the prosecution's job of presenting elements of murder, and the motive, much easier.

Brenda Lafferty

On July 24, 1984, Ron and Dan Lafferty, two self-proclaimed religious zealots, forcibly entered the home of their sister-in-law, Brenda Lafferty, who resided in American Fork, Utah. Outside, recent parolees Richard Knapp and Charles Carnes waited and watched from their parked vehicle. Once inside, the Lafferty brothers brutally beat and strangled Brenda Lafferty, leaving her bloodied, unconscious body in the kitchen. Dan Lafferty entered the bedroom of his 14-month-old niece, Erica, and spoke to the child briefly before cutting her throat from ear to ear, nearly severing her head from her body.

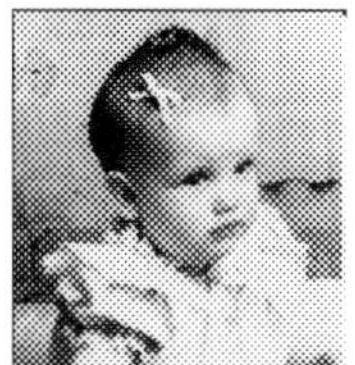
Erica Lafferty

Ronald Lafferty

In his own testimony at the re-trial of Ron Lafferty in 1996, Dan stated that he returned to the unconscious Brenda and "slit her throat" in a ritualistic manner similar to the baby. Calmly, the brothers washed their hands in the bathroom sink, cleaned their knife (or knives) on the curtains, and left the residence to go to the home of their next intended victim, Chloe Lowe. Fortunately, Mrs. Lowe wasn't at home, so they ransacked her home, breaking everything they could find. They then started for their final target, Richard Stowe, but missed the correct turn and decided to flee the area instead of returning to his residence. Eight hours after the slaying of Brenda and Erica, Alan Lafferty, the unsuspecting husband and father, returned home from work and discovered his murdered wife and child.

Dan Lafferty

Richard Knapp

The Laffertys were captured several weeks later. In a hushed news conference following the Lafferty arraignment on murder charges, Ron Lafferty spoke to members of the media, and referenced the extermination order he wrote regarding the need to "remove" Brenda, Erica and the others. Ron stated that "removed" didn't mean anything in particular, but the media would need to "pray about" the meaning if they wanted to know anything further. American Fork investigators correctly assumed though, that "removed," really meant to "murder." During the execution of several search warrants following the Lafferty brothers' arrests, the "removal" letter was recovered. In the letter, Ron penned the following, as if he were quoting a revelation from God:

"...For they have become obstacles in my path and I will not allow my work to be stopped. First thy brother's wife Brenda and her baby. It is my will that they be removed in rapid succession and that an example be made of them in order that others might see the fate of those who fight against the true saints of God. And it is my will that this matter be taken care of as soon as possible and I will prepare a way for my instrument to be delivered and instruction be given unto my servant...." (Removal document, 1984)

To most of us, the physical and forensic evidence is clear. Police must collect blood and fiber, fingerprints and still/video photographs. Diagrams of the crime scene, location and position of the victims and other pertinent items must be cataloged. The prosecutors in this case had to present the evidence in a manner that the jury could easily understand and have confidence in.

In order for any piece of evidence to be introduced into a criminal court, it must be shown that it was legally and appropriately obtained. The Fourth Amendment protects and serves as a basis for the manner in which a

THUS SAITH THE LORD UNTO MY SERVENTS THE PROPHETS. IT IS MY WILL AND COMMANDMENT THAT YE REMOVE THE FOLLOWING INDIVIDUALS IN ORDER THAT MY WORK MIGHT GO FORWARD. FOR THEY HAVE TRULY BECOME OBSTACLES IN MY PATH AND I WILL NOT ALLOW MY WORK TO BE STOPPED. FIRST THY BROTHER'S WIFE BRENDA AND HER BABY, THEN ████████, AND THEN ████████ AND IT IS MY WILL THAT THEY BE RE-MOVED IN RAPID SUCCESSION AND THAT AN EXAMPLE BE MADE OF THEM IN ORDER THAT OTHERS MIGHT SEE THE FATE OF THOSE WHO FIGHT AGAINST THE TRUE SAINTS OF GOD. AND IT IS MY WILL THAT THIS MATTER BE TAKEN CARE OF AS SOON AS POSSIBLE AND I WILL PREPARE A WAY FOR MY INSTRUMENT TO BE DELIVERED AND INSTRUCTION BE GIVEN UNTO MY SERVANT TODD. AND IT IS MY WILL THAT HE SHOW GREAT CARE IN HIS DUTIES FOR I HAVE RAISED HIM UP AND PREPARED HIM FOR THIS IMPORTANT WORK AND IS HE NOT LIKE UNTO MY SERVANT PORTER ROCKWELL. AND GREAT BLESSINGS AWAIT HIM IF HE WILL DO MY WILL, FOR I AM THE LORD THY

GOD AND HAVE CONTROL OVER ALL THINGS. BE STILL AND KNOW THAT I AM WITH THEE.

EVEN SO AMEN

person or property is legally seized. Reasonableness is the overriding test of compliance with the Fourth Amendment, and what constitutes "reasonableness" can vary according to the circumstances of the event (Zurcher v. Stanford Daily, 1978).

Since DNA was not a "household" name in the mid-1980's, blood was collected and matched to the victim and other crime scene participants by blood type only. Close examination of the crime scene revealed some pieces of valuable forensic evidence such as the damaged front door, cut vacuum cleaner and telephone cords, and one of the most valuable pieces of forensic evidence, the bloody curtains in the kitchen, where a perfect impression of the murder weapon was transferred as the knife was cleaned off. That impression was later used in the courtroom to show that a knife that Ron Lafferty purchased prior to the homicide and discarded alongside a road near Wendover, Nevada was the same piece of evidence that left the impression.

In addition to the physical evidence at the crime scene, investigators also recovered the "removal" revelation from a shirt pocket in Ron Lafferty's closet. This shirt was tied directly to Ron Lafferty by handwriting analysis and by showing family pictures where Ron was seen wearing the shirt in which the document was found. In addition, after their arrest, Charles Carnes and Richard Knapp provided evidence and testimony that supported the physical evidence in the case.

Let's look at the circumstantial evidence in this case. The Lectric Law Library's Lexicon describes circumstantial evidence this way: "Circumstantial evidence is best explained by saying what it is not - it is not direct evidence from a witness who saw or heard something. Circumstantial evidence is a fact that can be used to infer another fact" (Lectric Law, 2001).

The circumstantial evidence used in this case would focus primarily on the religious activities of the Lafferty brothers. For example, the note, wherein Ron indicates that Brenda and Erica must be "removed." The knife that was used to cut the throats of the victims was found on a roadside near Wendover, Nevada where the Laffertys were spotted a few days after the murders. The recovered knife, as noted earlier, was tied to Ron Lafferty via his purchase a few weeks before the murder at the "Cutlery" store in the University Mall in Provo, Utah and the testimony of Charles Carnes who testified about Ron Lafferty carrying the knife in his boot and throwing it away near Wendover after the murders.

> ***"Criminal behavior is the satisfaction of legitimate needs through illegitimate means."***
>
> Greg Cooper

While no one but Dan Lafferty could testify about Ron's use of the knife in the commission of the crime, it was circumstantially tied to the Laffertys. Other circumstantial evidence would come from associates of the Laffertys who would testify that the brothers had shared their revelation and intent to kill with them before the murders. Those witnessing this included Mrs. Lafferty (the mother of the Lafferty brothers), the victims' husband/ father and the other Lafferty brothers who participated in religious meetings with the two killers. Interestingly, everyone rejected the revelation and plan except Ron and Dan.

Thus we see that this indirect evidence implies something occurred but doesn't directly prove it. Proof of one or more facts from which one can find another fact or proof of a chain of facts and circumstances indicating that the person is either guilty or not guilty would appropriately describe circumstantial evidence (2001).

The next traditional form of evidence we will discuss is the eyewitness. Imagine this scenario that is played out in police academies across the country:

A classroom full of police recruits are listening to a crime scene instructor's lecture when all of a sudden a masked man enters the classroom, fires three shots at the instructor (who falls to the ground) and the gunman flees. Before the recruits can compose themselves and give pursuit, the instructor gets off the floor and tells the recruits that the shooting was a simulation. He then instructs the recruits to describe the gunman in detail, describe the weapon he used and the number of shots he fired. The answers might astound you. Chances are, if there were 20 recruits in the audience, you would get 20 different descriptions and answers. The question then is WHY?

Eyewitness accounts can be complicated by many factors. Lighting, distance, quality of eyesight, life experiences, prejudices and many other factors can affect how one might recall a situation, especially a stressful situation. Consider this scenario. "What color is a light blue 1977 Chevrolet 4-door when it's sitting under a streetlight at 2:00 in the morning?" As you think about this, you might take in to account the lighting, weather or other environmental conditions as you think this through. You might say that the car is white, silver, or perhaps even gray. Well, it's a trick question. A light blue 1977 Chevrolet 4-door, sitting under a streetlight at 2:00 in the morning, is still light blue, but our mind might be tricked into thinking it is an entirely different color, which would be wrong. This is a simple example, but the wrong piece of information from an eyewitness could lead an investigator or jury in the wrong direction, reducing the chances of solving the crime or convicting the offender.

In the case of the Laffertys, the eyewitnesses to the crime were Richard Knapp and Charles Carnes. They testified that they listened to the Lafferty brothers talking about killing Brenda and the others, they rode in Lafferty's vehicle to Brenda's residence, and they watched the brothers forcibly enter Brenda's home. A short time later, they witnessed as the brothers exited the victims' home, noting that they were "covered in blood." Once the brothers were in the car, they testified that they heard Ron say to Dan, "Thanks brother, I don't think I could have killed the kid," to which Dan replied, "No problem." (State v. Lafferty, 1985)

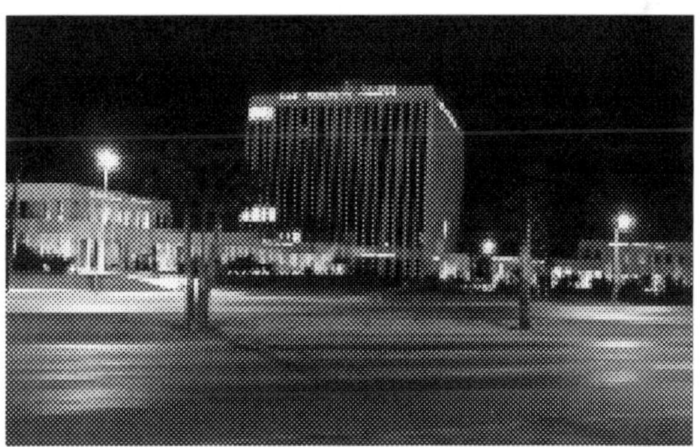

Of course, the favorite and last form of traditional evidence is the confession. Confessions are something that law enforcement officers hope for, prosecutors pray for, and defense attorneys cringe at the very mention of. Juries love to hear about confessions, because the confession can reduce the tremendous burden placed on the jury to determine truth. Unfortunately though, there have been circumstances when acquired confessions have been falsified. When a bizarre crime catches the media's attention, law enforcers are confronted with individuals who claim responsibility for the crime. To the stable mind, this may seem ludicrous, but to a person living a mundane life, it may give them the recognition for which they had hoped. Time and again, people have made this terrible decision for fame.

According to David E. Zulawski and Douglas E. Wicklander in the book <u>Practical Aspects of Interview and Interrogation</u>, an offender will only confess based on "...the decision whether the benefits of telling the truth outweigh the consequences resulting from an admission" (1993, pg. 110). In the Lafferty case, the brothers chose not to provide any statements to police and they didn't testify in their initial hearing or trial. Dan Lafferty later testified in the re-trial of his brother Ron, and while it appeared that he was adjusting his comments to assist his brother (primarily claiming sole responsibility for both murders), his testimony actually assisted prosecutors in convincing the court to find Ronald Lafferty guilty of murdering Brenda and Erica Lafferty, resulting in the issuance of the death penalty. Ron Lafferty is currently on death row and Dan is serving a life sentence without the possibility of parole. They are both housed in the Utah State Correctional Facility.

The final form of evidence that this paper will explore is behavior evidence. This is a relatively new investigative concept and thus it is referred to as the "new" form of evidence. While there has been little empirical study into the abilities that contribute to proficient performance in behavioral science as it applies to criminal investigations and prosecutions, it is clear that law enforcement has conducted these assessments or profiles informally for many years. "A study of behavior generally includes a review of an offender's traits, behavioral tendencies and demographic characteristics" (Criminal Psychology and Forensic Technology, 2001, pg. 80).

When studying behavior as part of the prosecutorial theme, it is necessary to carefully evaluate what is being communicated verbally and non-verbally. Gaining a clearer understanding of these communication methods can help a prosecutor more fully understand the offender/defendant personality characteristics, help in identifying a prosecutorial strategy and direct questioning of potential jurors. In addition, behavioral assessments can give the prosecutor insight into the types of expert witnesses that will be needed to appropriately present the case, and will be beneficial once the trial is complete in developing pre-sentence assessments.

In the Lafferty case, Ron and Dan claimed that their motivation for the crime was that they were following God's direction. In personal interviews with Dan Lafferty, the convicted murderer stated, "My choice was to either violate man's laws or God's. If I chose to follow God and kill Brenda and the baby, I am breaking man's laws. If I obey your [society's] laws, I offend God who commanded me to kill them because they were daughters of perdition. To me the choice was simple" (Lafferty, Dan, 2000).

This created some interesting hurdles for the prosecution to overcome. By analyzing the offender's behavior at the crime scene, including before and after the crime, prosecutors were able to convince the court that Ron Lafferty was angry with Brenda because she maintained a friendship with Ron's ex-wife. Evidence showed

R. Lafferty, 2001

D. Lafferty, 2001

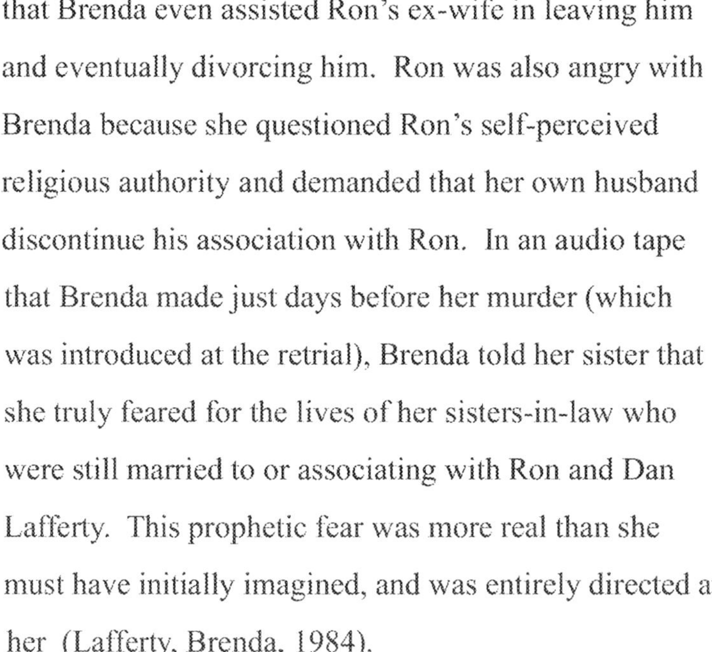

Carnes, 2001

Knapp, 2001

that Brenda even assisted Ron's ex-wife in leaving him and eventually divorcing him. Ron was also angry with Brenda because she questioned Ron's self-perceived religious authority and demanded that her own husband discontinue his association with Ron. In an audio tape that Brenda made just days before her murder (which was introduced at the retrial), Brenda told her sister that she truly feared for the lives of her sisters-in-law who were still married to or associating with Ron and Dan Lafferty. This prophetic fear was more real than she must have initially imagined, and was entirely directed at her (Lafferty, Brenda, 1984).

In the course of assaulting Brenda, Ron was overheard by Dan to say things that supported this claim. Dan recalled that Ron reacted violently to Brenda's plea for discontinuance of the assault. According to Dan, Brenda was bleeding so badly that she was slippery and Ron was having a hard time holding on to her as he struck her over and again. Brenda was overheard by Dan to say, "please Ron, I'll do anything, please just hold me." Ron replied, "I wish I had someone to hold after you @#$#-up my marriage you @#$%" (Lafferty, Dan, 2000).

This intense level of anger was used as an example to convince the jury that Ron was not acting out of righteous compulsion, and that his anger clearly showed a motive for murder by accentuating Ron's hatred to Brenda for breaking up his marriage. Further evidence that supported Ron was a murderer and not a religious zealot circled around the efforts to avoid detection that Ron made. He changed his name after the murders, traveled to several different states trying to escape, and to this day has never made any attempt to explain or accept his responsibility in the murders. Appropriately so, the courts ruled in favor of the prosecution, and the Laffertys, Carnes and Knapp were sentenced for the murders of Brenda and Erica.

Behavior, appropriate or inappropriate, is involuntary, quite dependable and is consistent with the sender's, (or defendant's) thoughts, feelings and emotions. It is reflective of suppressed motives and desires. Behavioral analysis employs a systematic approach. It is not witchery, but a process of applying principles, disciplines, experiences and education. It identifies and interprets the behavioral aspects of a crime in a manner that is easy to follow and translate.

Although behavioral analysis is a relatively new art form, it has been used in many difficult criminal cases to bring about a successful resolution. Formally starting in 1940 with the New York City Bomber case, the art has developed and progressed over time. In 1972, agents from the Federal Bureau of Investigations Behavioral Science Unit started to merge behavior and investigative science together as it was being taught at the FBI National Academy.

In 1977, Special Agents John Douglas and Robert Ressler convinced Bureau authorities of the need to further investigate the motivation behind serial crime (particularly homicide) in the United States, and they conducted a series of in-depth interviews with serial murderers across the country. In 1981, the notoriety of the Wayne B. Williams case (the Atlanta child murders)

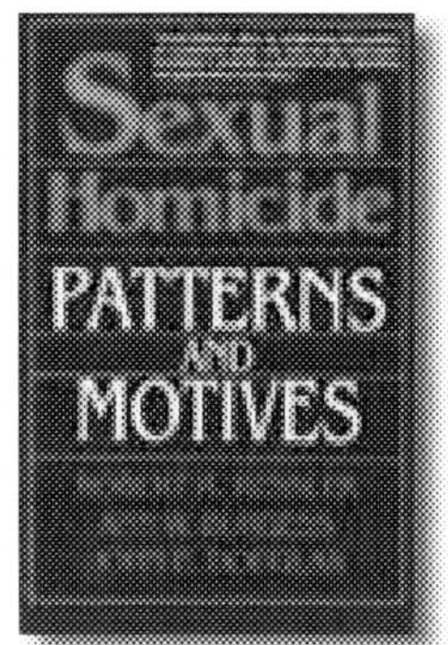

consumed the headlines of newsprint. John Douglas prepared the formalized profile that proved beneficial in the investigation and prosecution, where he ultimately testified in the government's behalf.

By the year 1985 the National Center for the Analysis of Violent Crime (NCAVC) standardized terminology in regard to behavior and the Violent Criminal Apprehension Program (ViCAP) became operational. During 1989 and 1991, the combined efforts of Douglas and Ressler's research resulted in the publication of

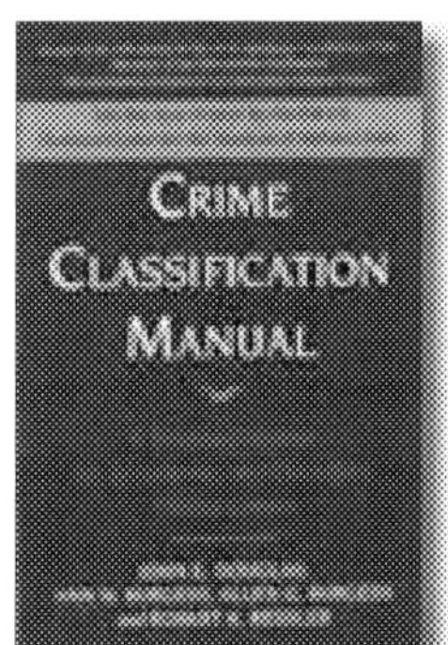

"Sexual Homicide: Patterns and Motives," by Douglas, Burgess, Burgess and Ressler and the "Crime Classification Manual" by Douglas, Burgess, Burgess and Ressler, respectively.

Those were the only two books stemming from the FBI unit efforts, but since that time many other experts have compiled documentation and resource material in this regard. Historically, law enforcement has investigated and presented cases for prosecution based on the four traditional forms of evidence. As the introduction of behavior becomes more commonplace, the quality and success of the investigation should improve, greatly enhancing the prosecution's job of presenting the case to the "people" who must then decide the fate of an offender/defendant.

References

Criminal Psychology and Forensic Technology (2001). <u>Criminal psychological profiling in violent crime investigations: a comparative assessment of accuracy</u>, Kocsis, Irwin, Hayes & Nunn. Boca Raton, Florida: CRC Press

Lectric Law Library (2001). <u>Circumstantial evidence</u>. Available: http://www.lectlaw.com

Lafferty, Brenda (1984). <u>Audio tape letter</u>. Utah.

Lafferty, Daniel (2000). <u>Personal interview</u>. Utah State Prison, Utah.

Marbury v. Madison (1803). 5 U.S. (1 Cranch) 137.

Morgan, B.K. (2000). <u>The authority and limitations of law enforcement power</u>, The Utah Prosecutor Handbook, Utah.

Removal Letter (1984). Ron Lafferty. Utah.

State v. Lafferty (1985) <u>Testimony given during trial</u>. Utah County, Utah.

Zulawski David E. & Wicklander, Douglas E. (1993). <u>Practical aspects of interview and interrogation</u>, New York: CRC Press.

Zurcher v. Stanford Daily (1978). 436 U.S. 547.

chapter review

What are the Four Traditional forms of Evidence?

1. ___________________________   2. ___________________________

3. ___________________________   4. ___________________________

What is the New Form of Evidence?   5. ___________________________

Name Four Characteristics of Behavioral Evidence.

1. ___________________________   2. ___________________________

3. ___________________________   4. ___________________________

- chapter five -

BEHAVIOR

Abstract

Criminal Investigative Analysis includes an analysis of specific behaviors unique to a criminal and his or her personality. It allows narrowing the list of possible offenders which may initially be quite large, to a much smaller list based on probabilities. This analysis increases the success, quality and speed of the criminal justice system. This chapter will focus on this process.

The process of criminal investigative analysis of behavior will focus on three primary areas;

1. Thought:	**Reasoning power-the power to imagine and fantasize (idea, metaphysical, nontangible).**
2. Feeling:	**A sensation of responding to stimuli through one of the five senses: touch, sight, smell, hearing, and taste.**
	A psychic and physical reaction subjectively experienced as strong feelings, and physiologically involving changes that prepare the body for immediate, vigorous action.
3. Emotion:	**A state of feeling in response or reaction to a person or situation.**

By directing our focus and investigative attention on the most probable suspect in a case, we can more quickly move the investigation along without wasting valuable time or putting other victims in jeopardy of a suspects continued criminal activity.

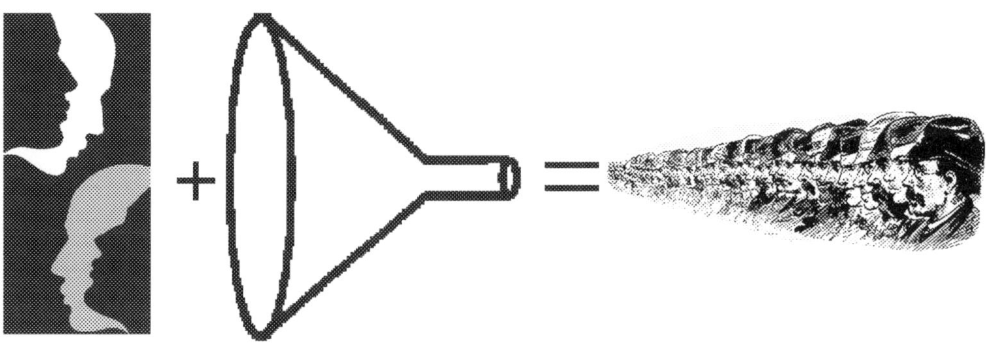

Deviant behavior is that behavior which contrasts or changes, especially from expected or acceptable standards such as a law, rule, or custom. It usually represents a significant departure from the norm. It is often described by such terms as abnormal, aberrant, or atypical.

Criminal behavior is defined as behavior that is in violation of the law. It also fits the definition of "deviant" behavior; however, the standard of measurement applied is defined by the law as "criminal."

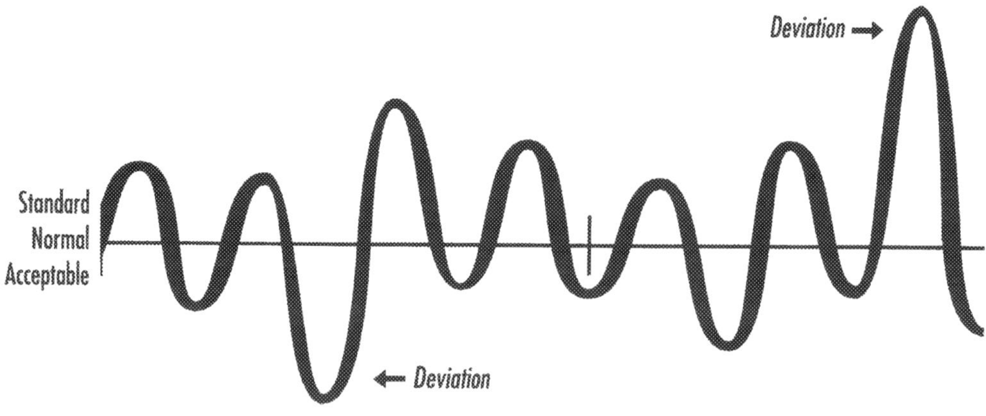

The standard of conduct on the "Behavioral Continuum," applied as a gauge, will impose certain consequences associated with variations to the acceptable standard.

> # Behavior: What is it?
> *Behavior is an expression of thought, feeling and emotion.*

There are three forms of behavior that are found either in part or whole at all crime scenes. They are:

1- **verbal,**
2- **nonverbal, and**
3- **sexual behavior.**

The verbal can be easily explained by the things said by the offender. The nonverbal could be a bizarre action(s) made or taken by the offender. Finally, the sexual would be any peculiar fantasies or actions required by the offender.

All criminals are motivated by physiological and learned motives. Physiological motives are activities that are characteristic of, or appropriate to, a person's healthy or normal functioning. Learned motives might be aggression, affiliation and achievement. Aggression would be defined in this example as a forceful action or procedure (as an unprovoked attack), especially when intended to dominate or master another person. It is generally hostile, injurious and destructive behavior that occurs out of anger or frustration.

Affiliation, or motivation because of belonging to a gang or group, can lead to motive, just so the criminal can belong to something. Affiliation can give a person living an otherwise mundane life a special feeling of superiority or partnership in something. The desire to achieve, to be the best at something, to have power or dominion, is a terrific motivator for good or evil.

Fundamental Theories of Human Behavior and Motivation

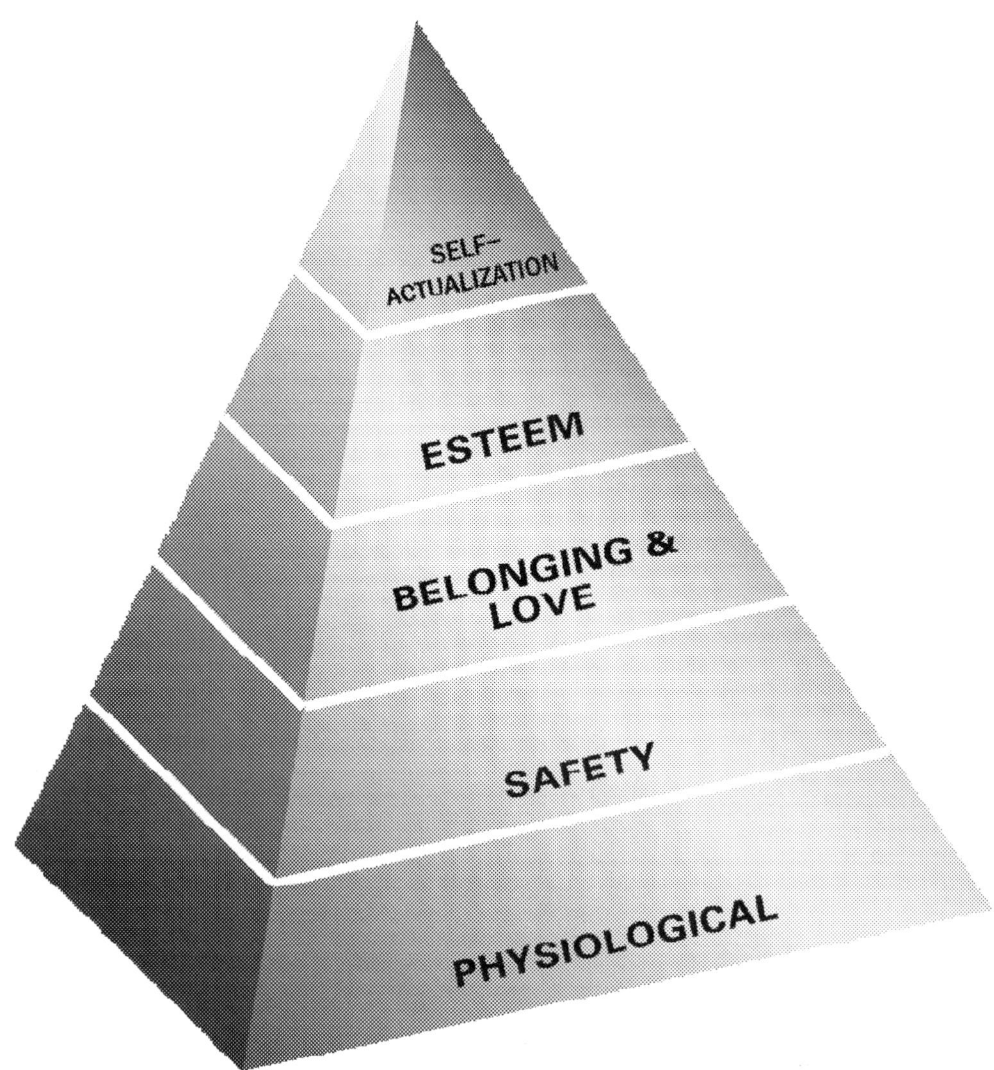

MASLOW'S HIERARCHY OF NEEDS

Professor Davis at the University of Toledo, recapped Abraham Maslow's Hierarchy of Needs in the following manner;

"A member of the Chicago dynasty of psychologists and sociologists, Abraham Maslow published his theory of human motivation in 1943. Its popularity continues unabated. Like his colleague Carl Rogers, Maslow believed that actualization was the driving force of human personality, a concept he captures in his 1954 book, <u>Motivation and Personality.</u>

"A musician must make music, an artist must paint, a poet must write, if he is to be ultimately at peace with himself. What a man can be, he must be."

Maslow's great insight was to place actualization into a hierarchy of motivation. Self actualization, as he called it, is the highest drive, but before a person can turn to it, he or she must satisfy other, lower motivations like hunger, safety and belonging. The hierarchy has five levels.

1. Physiological (hunger, thirst, shelter, sex, etc.)

2. Safety (security, protection from physical and emotional harm)

3. Social (affection, belonging, acceptance, friendship)

4. Esteem (also called ego). The internal ones are self respect, autonomy, achievement, and the external ones are status, recognition, attention.

5. Self actualization (doing things)

Maslow points out that the hierarchy is dynamic; the dominant need is always shifting. For example, the musician may be lost in the self actualization of playing music, but eventually becomes tired and hungry so he or she has to stop. Moreover, a single behavior may combine several levels. For example, eating dinner is both physiological and social. The hierarchy does not exist by itself, but is affected by the situation and the general culture. Satisfaction is relative. Finally, he notes that a satisfied need no longer motivates. For example, a hungry man may be desperate for food, but once he eats a good meal, the promise of food no longer motivates him.

This highly popular theory strikes most people as intuitively right. Douglas McGregor makes it the building block for his Theory X and Theory Y. Mihalyi Csikszentmihalyi continues the tradition in his concept of "flow." A 1990's example of self actualization may be surfing the Internet. Empirical research has confirmed the first three levels, but has not done so for the fourth and fifth levels of esteem and self actualization.

Some have noted that Maslow's hierarchy follows the life cycle. A newborn baby's needs are almost entirely physiological. As the baby grows, it needs safety, then love. Toddlers are eager for social interaction. Teenagers are anxious about social needs, young adults are concerned with esteem, and only more mature people transcend the first four levels to spend much time self actualizing.

James K. Van Fleet, in "Conversation Skill Builder Guidebook" (Nightingale-Conant) described fourteen human motivators that impact our decision making. They are:

Sense of personal power and mastery of others

Sense of pride and importance

Financial security and success

Reassurance of self-worth and recognition of efforts

Peer approval and acceptance

Desire to win, to excel, to be the best

Sense of belonging to either a place or a group

Opportunity for creative self-expression

Accomplishment of something worthwhile

New experiences

Sense of individual liberty and freedom

Sense of self-esteem, dignity and self-respect

Experience of love in all forms

Emotional security

The elements of personality are affected by our biological makeup, i.e., our genes and gender, and the experiences we have in our lives, i.e., family, culture and environment. Personality can be best described as an individual's characteristic pattern of behavior, thought, and emotion.

> **Personality Disorder: What is it?**
>
> *A failure of the personality itself to develop, adjust and learn.*

Sigmund Freud, the father of psychoanalysis, suggested that the psyche, or mind, consists of three structures: the id, superego, and ego. We are unaware of these structures, but they determine much of our behavior.

The id is thought to be the primitive part of the psyche. It is the part of us that we are born with and it is driven by animal instincts. Freud argued that the id functions according to the pleasure principle, in that it seeks to maximize pleasure and minimize discomfort; it is illogical in its drive for what feels good and is fun.

The superego is that part of the psyche that is driven by the desire to be moral and good. It is thought to form in early childhood when we become aware of cultural norms and societal standards. The superego is our sense of conscience and functions according to the morality principle. It is just as illogical as the id because it seeks what is moral and right above all else.

The third part of the psyche is the ego. It is our sense of self and develops during toddlerhood as we begin to seek autonomy from our parents. The ego is a sort of executive control center because it can control the id and superego. Its job is to seek a balance between the conflicting desires of the id

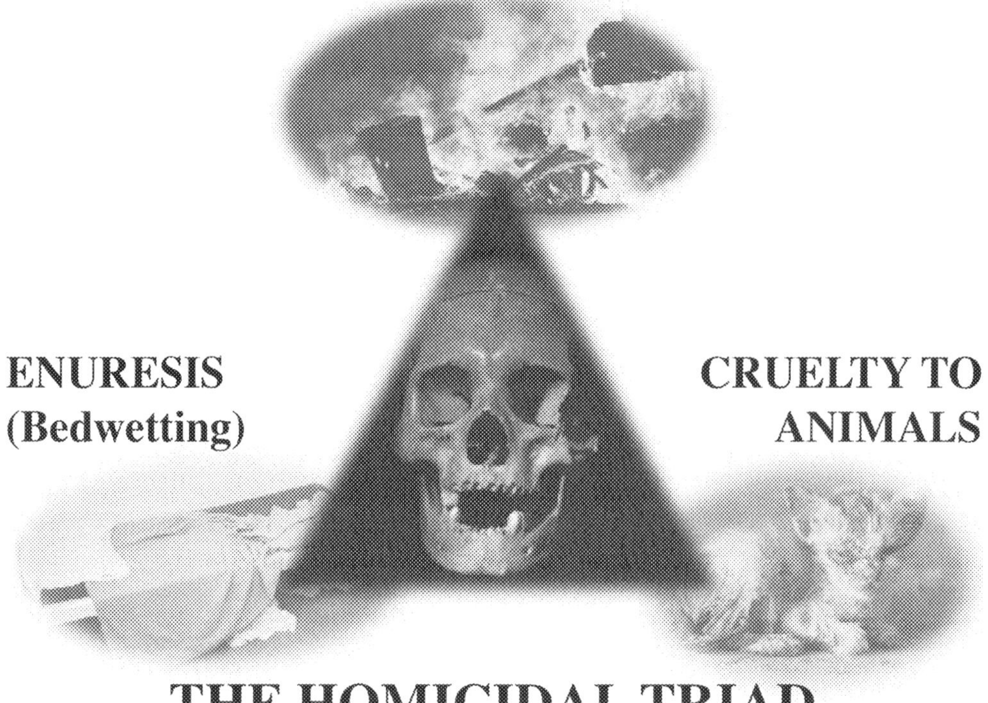

THE HOMICIDAL TRIAD

and superego. It seeks to gratify the id's desire for pleasure in accord with the superego's desire for what is moral. Although we are not aware of the id, ego, and superego, Freud believed that the conflicts and interactions among the three structures determine much of our behavior.

Criminal Personality: What is it?

An individual's characteristic pattern of behavior, thought and emotion which is expressed through criminal conduct (violation of the law).

On the other side of personality is criminal personality, which can be defined as an individual's characteristic pattern of behavior, thought, and emotion which is expressed through criminal conduct (violation of the law).

A "psychopath" is a *term associated with a specific personality disorder. The* DSM Manual IV definition for "antisocial personality disorder":

A. There is a pervasive pattern of disregard for and violation of the rights of others occurring since age 15, as indicated by three (or more) of the following:

> 1) Failure to conform to social norms with respect to lawful behaviors as indicated by repeatedly performing acts that are grounds for arrest
>
> 2) Deceitfulness, as indicated by repeated lying, use of aliases, *or* conning others for personal profit or pleasure
>
> 3) Impulsivity or failure to plan ahead
>
> 4) Irritability and aggressiveness, as indicated by repeated physical fights or assaults
>
> 5) Reckless disregard for safety of self or others
>
> 6) Consistent irresponsibility, as indicated by repeated failure to sustain consistent work behavior or honor financial obligations

7) Lack of remorse, as indicated by being indifferent to or rationalizing having hurt, mistreated, or stolen from another

B. The individual is at least 18

C. There is evidence of "conduct disorder" with onset before age 15

D. The occurrence of antisocial behavior is not exclusive to the course of schizophrenia or a manic episode

The illustration to the right reflects the general nature of a psychopath.

PSYCHOPATH

CRUEL	**C**UNNING
HATE	**H**ABITUAL CRIMINAL
AMORAL	**A**CTOR
MANIPULATIVE	**M**ACHO
EGO	**E**GOTISTIC
LONER, LIAR	**L**OW FRUSTRATION TOLERANCE
EVIL	**E**XPERIMENTATION
OVERT	**O**PERATOR
NOCTURNAL	**N**O GUILT

Behavioral Model

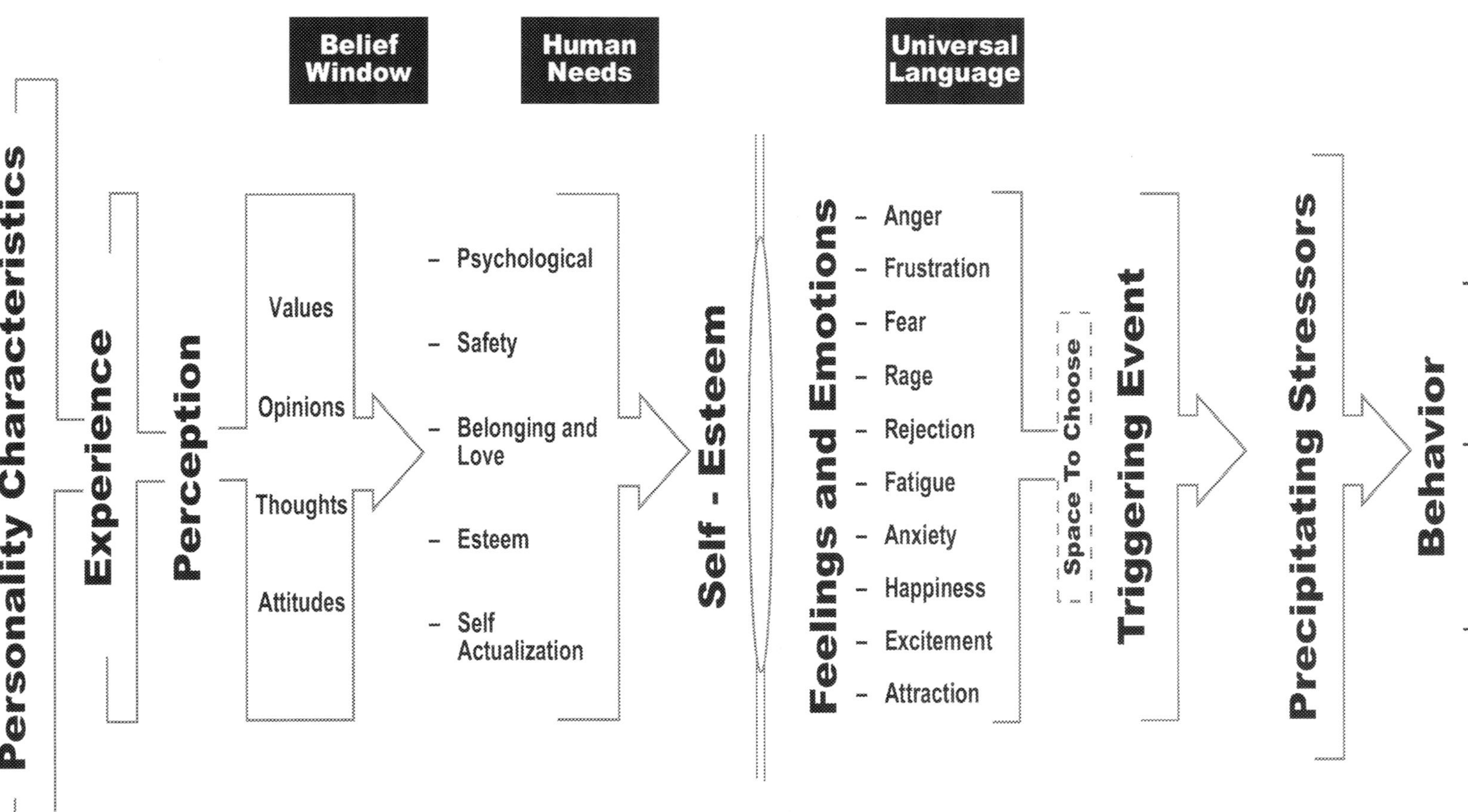

chapter review

What are the three forms of behavior?

Define Physiological Motivation?

Name at least three Learned Motives?

What is Personality?

What are two Influencing Factors of personality and explain?

chapter six

INTERPERSONAL COMMUNICATION

Abstract

Interpersonal communication is the process of communication between at least two people interacting and influencing each other. The most dramatic form of interpersonal communication is exchanged during the commission of interpersonal violence. The following models effectively diagram criminal behavior while illustrating the associated communication elements.

The BTK case demonstrates the application of behavioral and communication principles for the purpose of criminal investigation and analysis. The offender communicates with the investigative team through his behavior. Identifying and analyzing the communication from the offender will provide clues to his personality and possible identity. The communication is

> **"It is the recipient who communicates. The so-called communicator, the person who emits the communication, does not communicate. He utters. Unless there is someone who hears, there is no communication. There is only noise. The communicator speaks or writes or sings—but he does not communicate. Indeed, he cannot communicate. He can only make it possible, or impossible, for a recipient—or rather, "percipient"—to perceive."**
>
> Peter F. Drucker
> Management: Tasks,
> Responsibilities, Practices
> Horper and Row, 1974

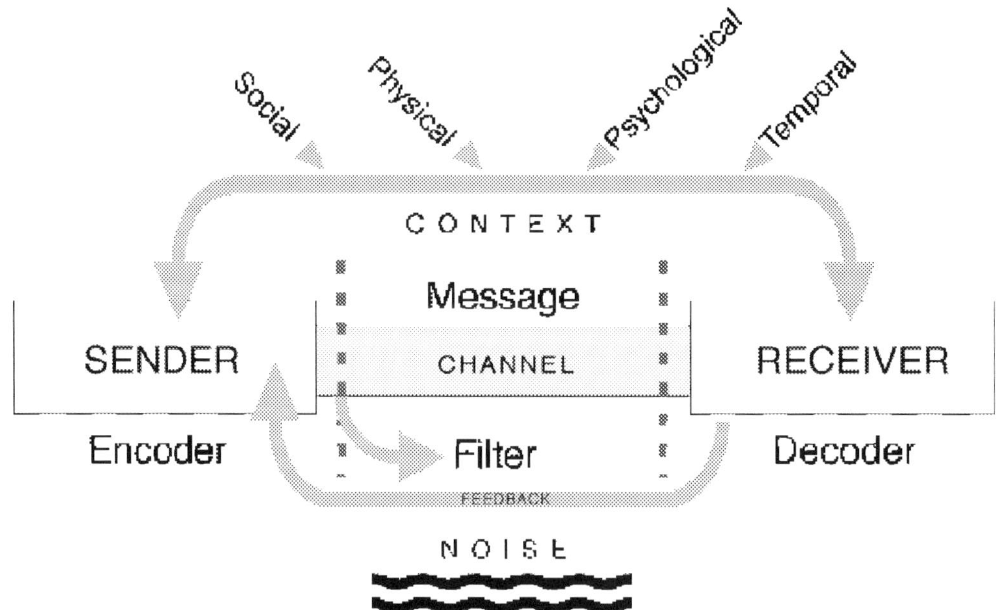

Elements of the Interpersonal Communication Model

1. **Sender:** **The person sending the information.**

2. **Receiver:** **The person receiving the information.**

3. **Message:** **Expression of a thought, feeling or emotion by the sender (encoder).**

4. **Channel:** **Mode or means of transmission to the receiver (decoder) of the thought, feeling or emotion.**

5. **Filter:** **Screening process by both the sender and receiver to translate/interpret the message into a meaningful form.**

6. **Noise:** **Anything that distorts or interfers with the message.**

7. **Context:** **The setting of the communication.**

8. **Feedback:** **Response from the decoder processing the information.**

The Four Dimensions of "Context"

1. **Physical:** **Tangible or concrete environment.**
2. **Social:** **Status or relationship among participants.**
3. **Psychological:** **Friendliness or unfriendliness of the situation.**
4. **Temporal:** **Time**

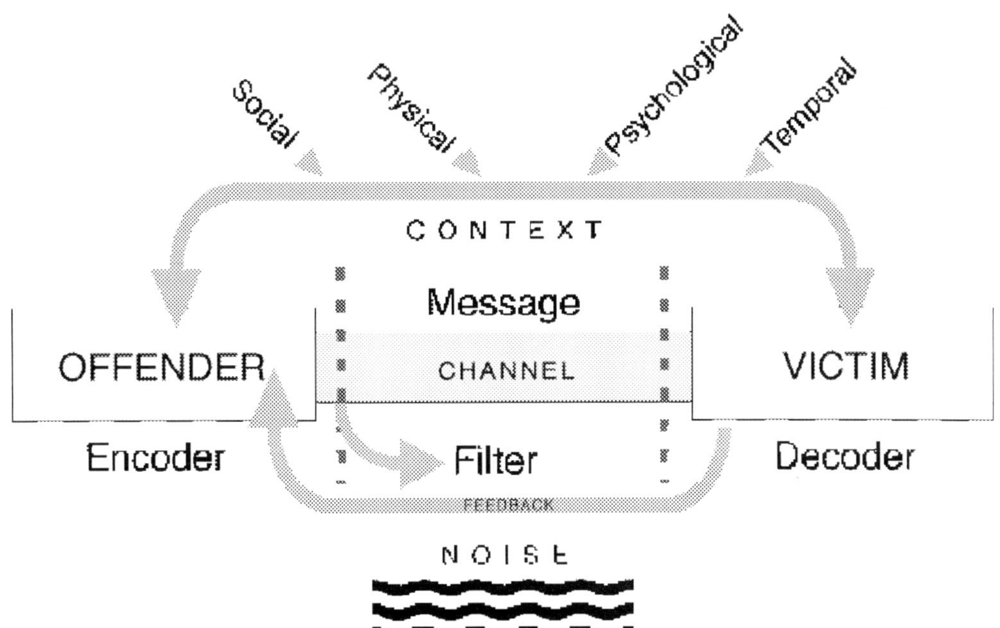

Elements of the Interpersonal Violence Model

1. **Sender:**   **Offender.**

2. **Receiver:**   **Victim.**

3. **Message:**   **Motive (why?)**

4. **Channel:**   **MO (verbal, nonverbal, sexual), weapon(s).**

5. **Filter:**   **Situation, circumstance, environment (psychological or physical).**

6. **Noise:**   **Distortions, distractions, inhibitions, (response of victim, phone calls, etc.)**

7. **Context:**   **Initial contact site, crime scene, disposal site.**

8. **Feedback:**   **Defense wounds.**

The Four Dimensions of "Context"

1. **Physical:**   **Primary location of communication.**
2. **Social:**   **Social relationship between victim and offender.**
3. **Psychological:**   **Emotional relationship between victim and offender.**
4. **Temporal:**   **Crucial times (contact between victim and offender, last time victim was seen, approximate time of death, etc.)**

reflected in three ways: verbal (written letters), nonverbal (photographs), and sexual (sexual assault). As you read the case, reflect on the three types of criminal behavior discussed and indicate the characteristics and behavior on the chart below.

Characteristic	Verbal	Non	Sex

THE BTK CASE: "The BTK Strangler"
"Bind - Torture - Kill"

Wichita, Kansas
courtesy of apbnews.com

Julie Otero

Between 1974 and 1977 an individual describing himself in letters to the media and police as the BTK (Bind, Torture and Kill) Strangler killed six, possibly seven people.

The first killing occurred Jan. 15, 1974, when 15-year-old Charlie Otero came home from school and discovered the bodies of his 11-year-old sister, Josephine, his 9-year-old brother, Joseph II, and his mother and father. All the victims were strangled by ligature -- the material used was left on their necks -- and all the victims were bound. Some of the family members were gagged. Josephine was hanging, lynch-like, from a pipe in the basement and was partially undressed. According to Capt. Paul Dotson of the Wichita Police Department, there was semen throughout the house.

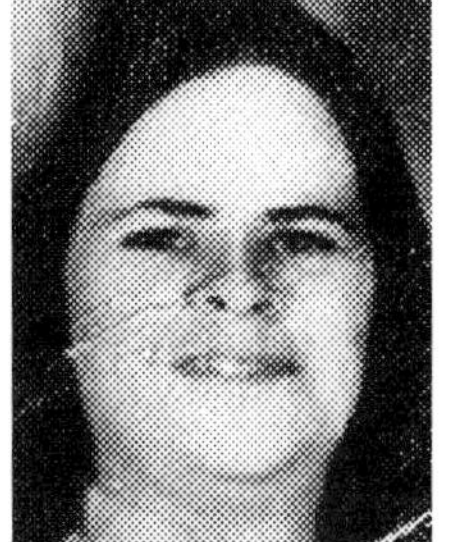

Shirley Vian

Nancy Fox

On March 17, 1977, 26-year-old Shirley Vian was found bound and strangled by ligature in her home. The ligature was also left on her neck. She was found in her bedroom, partially undressed. The incident occurred during the daytime, and there was no sign of forced entry.

Kathryn Bright

On Dec. 8, 1977, 25-year-old Nancy Fox was found in her home, killed by ligature strangulation. She was gagged, and her hands and feet were bound. She was found in her bedroom partially undressed. The crime occurred at night, and the offender gained entry through a broken window. Semen was found at the scene, but Fox wasn't sexually assaulted.

On April 4, 1974, 21-year-old Kathryn Bright was found in her home, stabbed three times in her stomach. She was bound, there was ligature activity around her neck, and she was partially undressed. Dotson said some detectives believe the Bright killing was also the work of the BTK Strangler. According to *The Wichita Eagle* newspaper, the offender referred to an unnamed victim (presumably Bright) in a letter he sent to the paper in February 1978.

The *Eagle* reported that the last confirmed incident involving the BTK Strangler occurred April 28, 1979, when he waited inside a house for the 63-year-old owner to show up, apparently targeting her daughter. He left after he grew tired of waiting. He later wrote a letter explaining this activity, according to investigators quoted in the paper.

In the late 1980s, the slaying of another family in the area and the killing of a young girl sparked off another flurry of letters to the police and media indicating these crimes were all committed by the BTK Strangler. Police believe they are not connected.

On Oct. 31, 1987, the body of 15-year-old Shannon Olson was found dumped in a pond in an industrial area, partially disrobed and stabbed numerous times.

On Dec. 31, 1987, Mary Fager, the married mother of two daughters, returned to her Wichita house from 2 1/2 days out of town. She found her husband shot twice in his back, killed while he was on his knees, according to Lt. Ken Landwehr of the Wichita Police Department. Her two daughters, Kelli, 16, and Sherri, 10, were both found strangled in the hot tub in the basement. Sherri's hands and feet were bound with black electrical tape.

According to Landwehr, William Butterworth, a local contractor, told police he went to the Fager house, where he was doing construction work, and discovered the father's body. He said he heard something in the house and fled in the family's car. He himself was reported missing Dec. 29. He was arrested four days later in Florida. According to Landwehr, Butterworth claimed he had amnesia. A jury acquitted Butterworth. Landwehr said they have closed the Fager case because they are convinced Butterworth is the killer. Butterworth's whereabouts today are unknown.

All the victims lived within approximately five miles of each other. The letter detailing the Otero killings was found inside the pages of a mechanical engineering book at the Wichita Public Library. Police received a tip to look there. They assume it was from the offender.

The *Eagle* reported and the police confirmed that a poem about Vian was sent to the paper and that the poem was patterned after "Curley Locks," a children's poem that had recently appeared in Games, a puzzle magazine.

The *Eagle* reported it received a poem about Nancy Fox titled "Oh Death to Nancy," patterned after a poem called "Oh Death." Law enforcement has not released the BTK Strangler's letters to the public. When asked to characterize them, Dotson said, "Here I am. Pay attention."

Police said semen was found at both the Otero and Fox crime scenes, but Dotson said they haven't released whether the semen is the same. The media has reported and police have confirmed that the semen found is the type found in fewer than 6 percent of all males. Police won't release what type that is, citing rules of evidence.

A call was made to 911 to report the Nancy Fox killing. Police assume it was the offender. The tape was recorded.

Police also won't release whether the restraints used in the various homicides were the same material.   The case is still open.

chapter review

Define the Process of Communication.

In the Interpersonal Violence Model, the Sender is referred to as the

_________________________ and the Receiver is the _________________________.

Name the four Dimensions of Context in the Communication Model.

Identify one of the three forms of communication most often referred to in the Otero homicides and explain why you picked the specific communication form.

- chapter seven -

CRIMINAL INVESTIGATIVE ANALYSIS

Abstract

An inductive investigative procedure, the foundation to criminal investigative analysis is a comprehensive examination of the offender's specific behavior during the commission of a crime. While human behavior is a response to stimuli produced by thoughts, feelings, and emotions, it represents a universal language commonly understood. This common language allows the investigators to interpret the behavior from the offender's perspective and take the initial steps toward leading the investigation to a successful resolution.

Criminal investigative analysis is best viewed as a strategy enabling law enforcement to narrow the field of options and generate educated opinions about the identity of the offender. It involves identifying, analyzing, and interpreting the behavior of the offender to help identify a motive and formulate the characteristics of the offender. It is a proactive approach to increase the effectiveness and efficiency of the investigation.

Criminal Investigative Analysis: What is it?

Criminal Investigative Analysis is a study and analysis of the secret life committed in a private setting and exposed to public scrutiny and evaluation.

There are many key services that can be performed through criminal investigative analysis. By beginning the examination at the crime scene, and continually evaluating and re-examining the evidence through the final arguments in the courtroom, we can greatly enhance the quality and scope of criminal investigations.

> *"Behavior is a mirror in which everyone displays his own image."*
> Goethe
> Elective Affinities

The ground level services may include, but not necessarily be limited to, effective crime analysis, providing descriptions of offender characteristics, investigative strategies, interviewing techniques, search warrant information, prosecutorial strategies, expert witness testimony, pre-sentence assessments and threat assessments. *(refer to the UTAP model in chapter two for a more detailed description of each of these services.)*

The successful process of criminal investigative analysis involves four critical elements:

1) What we <u>view</u>,

2) What we <u>observe</u>,

3) How we <u>analyze</u> the data, and

4) The manner in which we <u>interpret</u> the data

There is great wisdom found in the quote by Sir Arthur Conan Doyle (Sherlock Holmes) in "A Scandal in Bohemia" (1891), who said, *"I have no data yet. It is a capital mistake to theorize before one has data. Insensibly one begins to twist the facts to suit the theories, instead of the theories to suit the facts."* Unfortunately, there are tragic examples in the media every day where law enforcement has been shown to have wrongly accused individuals, or worse, criminal courts have wrongly convicted innocent people of crimes. Sometimes the truth isn't discovered for many years after the fact and the real perpetrators go unpunished while an innocent person falls victim to a poor investigation.

Let's take a moment and explore the definition of each of these critical processes and how they apply to criminal cases. In each case, we will look at the generic meaning for the action, and then its application to criminal investigative analysis. (Definitions taken in part from the <u>Encarte on-line Encyclopedia</u> - 2001)

> ***"I have no data yet. It is a capital mistake to theorize before one has data. Insensibly one begins to twist the facts to suit the theories, instead of the theories to suit the facts."***
>
> Sir Arthur Conan Doyle
> (Sherlock Holmes)
> <u>A Scandal in Bohemia</u> (1891)

View: (noun) that comes from the 15th century. From Old French vëue , past participle of vëoir "to see," from Latin videre "to see" (source of English vision and voyeur). View involves the act of looking at, or inspecting something. It is also used when discussing a range of vision, i.e., "As we rounded the bend the mountains came into view." It is sometimes referred to as a scene or an area that can be seen from a particular place, especially one that is pleasing or impressive, a pictorial representation, perspective or opinion. For the purpose of criminal

investigative analysis we use the reference of "looking at, or inspecting" a crime scene or behavior. (This is a <u>verb</u> usage.)

Observe: (verb) originated in the 14th century. Via Old French observer from Latin observare, literally "to watch toward," from servare "to watch, pay attention." Observe is best defined as to notice, to see or notice something, especially while watching carefully, especially for scientific purposes. To be a formal witness or one who watches without taking part. In criminal investigative analysis, it is the next level of merely viewing a crime scene. We are not only looking and inspecting, but we are paying close attention to what we see. We are drawing on our experience, education and training to gain a deeper understanding of what is being communicated.

Analyze: (verb) With its ties to the early 17th century was possibly a back-formation from analysis, or from French analyse "analysis". To examine closely. To better understand. For the investigator, this important step will often provide insight into the offender's mind set. By breaking down a crime scene into components, we find out what something is made up of by identifying its many intriguing parts, often in great detail in order to understand it better or discover more about it.

Interpret: (verb) 14th century. Directly or via French "interpréter" from Latin "interpretari" - to explain. To establish or explain the meaning or significance of something or to ascribe a particular meaning or significance of something. To translate what is said in one language into another so that speakers of different languages can communicate. In the world of criminal investigative analysis, the profiler or behavioral analyst establishes the meaning of the forms of communication exhibited in a crime scene. The analyst may be called upon to translate what the crime scene may tell us about the offender's personality, level of experience in this particular crime, and the amount of organization that can be inferred based on the physical, circumstantial and behavioral evidence.

Processing a crime scene in the manner just described is one thing, processing the personality behavior of those involved is entirely different. There are three portions of a person's life that need to be discussed and better understood before progressing further. Often, when a person is charged by police for a criminal act, especially a high-profile person, there is an uproar in the community. On one side of the "fence" are those individuals who revel in someone else's demise or misfortune. They are quick to write in the "Letter to the Editor" section, condemning the individual. Invariably, on the other side of the fence are people who are close to the alleged perpetrator.

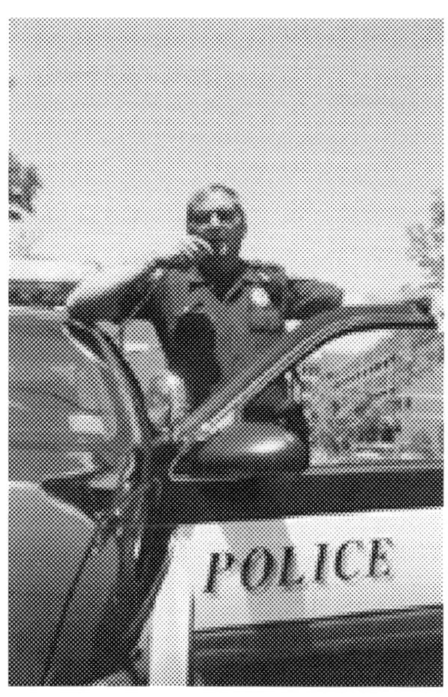

These individuals might be family members, neighbors, co-workers, or associates from clubs and churches. These individuals too might embark on a letter-writing campaign where they claim dismay at the unwarranted and wrongful charges brought forward. They share comments like, "He is the best neighbor I've ever had," or "He has always taken the time to work with our scouts and young people." Both sides of the "fence," so to speak, are correct *(based on their experience with the individual charged)* in their thinking. During a criminal justice event, police, prosecutors, victims and judges may hear account after account from concerned associates challenging the evidence, based on their personal experience with the defendant. The job of the police and prosecution then must be to carefully evaluate the alleged criminal's public, private and secret life.

Public Life: A person's public life is much easier to judge. This is the man or woman who works in our cities or towns, serves on community councils, volunteers as a youth coach or attends the local church. This is the public presentation he or she makes and the perceived personality type that they are. In public, we can develop opinions about them based on what we see them do, day in and day out. This is the person's life we hear about whenever there has been this division spoken of earlier. A good example might be the stellar member of the community who fights for "truth, justice and the American way," yet is addicted to prescription drugs, or is abusive in his home. To the public scrutiny, he is exemplary – when in reality he violates the law. Now, it must also be said that the public life persona is an accurate representation of the person's true personality, and gaining full understanding of this would be of great benefit to this type of person.

Private Life: A person's private life, as in the example above, may be much different. In the example of private life, one may be entirely different than he is perceived in his public life. For instance, a professional butler, who is known for his proper etiquette, cleanliness and appearance in public, may be a complete slob in the privacy of his own home. His house or apartment may be unkempt, with old pizza boxes and soda cans lying around the rooms, sometimes for days

on end. The individual he is in the
privacy of his own home, or on vacation,
or away from work, may be entirely
different than what he purports to be at
the office.

Stephen R. Covey
The Seven Habits of Highly
Effective People

Secret Life: A person's secret life is an interesting area of its own. This is where the secret thoughts occur, the fantasies or the deviance is born. When acted upon, these fantasies can become the unthinkable crimes we read about and are repulsed by. It is here that loved ones develop their individual fence lines. Too often, we place our own moral standards on others and hope that they too would feel as we about committing certain acts. Because it is too difficult to imagine an associate or loved one involved in these kinds of acts, we come to their defense, rather than trying to better understand both sides of the issue.

In order to effectively view, observe, analyze and interpret an offender's behavior at a crime scene, we must first gain as much information about the perpetrator as possible. If there are several suspects in a case, it is helpful to break the suspect information down into twenty-two "Offender Profile Characteristics." They are:

1. **Age**
2. **Sex**
3. **Race**
4. **Marital status / adjustment**
5. **Intelligence**

6. **Scholastic achievement / adjustment**
7. **Life-style**
8. **Rearing environment**
9. **Social adjustment**
10. **Personality style / characteristics**
11. **Demeanor**
12. **Appearance and grooming**
13. **Emotional adjustment**
14. **Evidence of mental decomposition**
15. **Pathological behavior characteristics**
16. **Employment / occupational history and adjustment**
17. **Work habits**
18. **Residency in relation to crime**
19. **Socio economic status**
20. **Type of sexual perversion or disturbance** *(if applicable)*
21. **Prior criminal arrest history**
22. **Motive**

The investigator's approach to analyzing and interpreting the offender's behavior is similar to a physician who applies a systematic procedure to assess the patient's symptoms and prescribe the cure. This orderly design facilitates an accurate diagnosis of both the offender's and the victim's behavior, and the subsequent appropriate investigative techniques to increase the chances of a successful resolution.

Imagine going to the dentist for your semi-annual checkup and teeth cleaning. As you sit down in the chair, your dentist pulls his mask over his face and puts a large grinding bit into his high speed drill. Without a word, he pulls out a large needle and focuses his attention on your mouth, bringing the needle ever closer. In desperation, you stop him and ask him what he is doing, to which he responds that he is numbing your mouth so that he can extract your molar. You tell him that you are only there to get your teeth cleaned and that there is nothing wrong with your molar. He states, "Well, my last patient needed his molar removed, I guess I just thought you needed the same thing."

Hopefully, at this point you are walking out of his office with a torn out copy of the yellow pages – intent on finding a new dentist. Our hope is that our dentists, and investigators, would 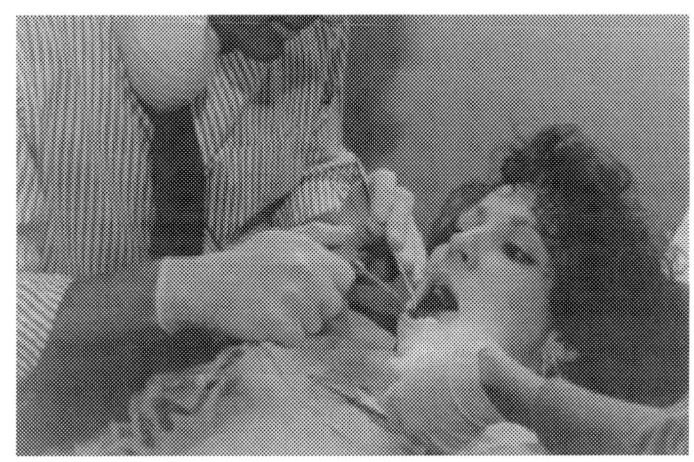 choose to follow this valuable advice from Stephen R. Covey in his book, "The Seven Habits of Highly Effective People." Covey taught us to "diagnose before you prescribe." How does this apply to criminal investigative analysis? Too often, investigators decide what the motive was for a crime long before they have fully investigated the crime. Too often, investigators question witnesses and suspects before they have fully prepared for the interview.

NEVER, "PRESCRIBE BEFORE YOU DIAGNOSE!"

To ensure greater success, the investigator must take the time to completely compile and review all of the investigative reports, from the initial response through follow-up interviews, medical examiner reports, and even media coverage. After doing this, he will be in a much better position to evaluate the behavior of the victim and the perpetrator.

It is very helpful to have as many crime scene photographs as possible taken and available to you at all times throughout the investigation. The crime scene photos could tip the investigator off to problems with suspect or witness statements or forensic findings. In regard to the victim, it is important the photographs focus on the wounds and the extent of the wounds. Close-up and panoramic photographs are very important so that any investigator who is

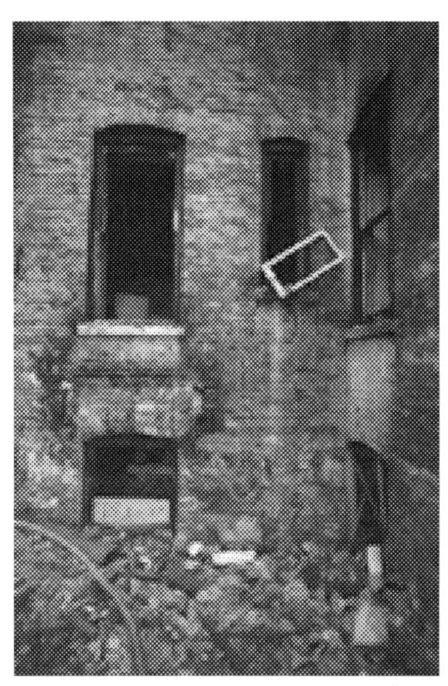

assigned to the case can better familiarize himself. It is helpful to show the position of the victim's body (s) from several different angles. If the crime scene is inside, all angles should be taken of the location, including other rooms, doorways, entrances, exits, etc. (Include a sketch or floor plan of the building that is to scale whenever possible.)

The exterior of the location and its relationship to the surrounding area should be photographed and any specific landmarks, entrances and exits from the area should be indicated and photographed. Aerial shots are very valuable and they should show the relationship of the crime scene, dump sites and other evidence to important landmarks. Make sure to include some type of distance measure on these photographs. Officers should be assigned whenever possible to closely monitor the area surrounding the crime scene during the investigation. These officers should watch for vehicles parked in the area, showing their location and license numbers, as well as any individuals or crowds that may gather *(Occasionally the offender returns to observe the police at work.)*

When examining the medical examine'rs reports, pay close attention to toxicology reports, and look for things like drugs, alcohol, hair cut off, the presence of semen, etc. Take time to interview the medical examiner to get any opinions or comments that might not otherwise have been committed to a report. Gain an understanding of why the suspect inflicted the types of injuries to the victim, both forensically and practically. Talk with individuals who knew the victim and create a map of the victim's travels and activities prior to death. This information should include where the victim works and lives, the location where the victim was last seen alive, and the location of the crime scene and disposal or discovery site.

Conduct a thorough Victimology study as described in chapter 7-1 (refer to chapter 7, section one for a complete listing of important components of a victimology study.) Assess the neighborhood and surrounding areas of each significant site pertaining to the crime. Determine what could have happened at each site and ensure that proper crime scene processing is completed.

> *"I keep six honest serving men (They taught me all I knew); Their names are What and Why and When And How and Where and Who."*
>
> Rudyard Kipling
> The Elephant's Child, 1902

Conduct a simple case review with other members of your staff and agency. Draw from the cumulative years of experience and expertise. Re-visit the case information from time to time in very detailed meetings. Invite trusted investigators who are unfamiliar with the case to sit in. They may present a "fresh" approach. They are not cluttered with the emotions of the case, and may not have the tunnel vision of those who have "lived" with the case since its occurrence. In those case reviews, hypothesize the scenario and sequence of events. Put yourself in the position of the victim and the offender. Identify possible motives and come up with the answers to the *Who, What, When, Where, How,* and *Why* questions. Consider the "crime classification" (from the *Crime Classification*

Manual) and formulate a profile of the offender personality characteristics (if applicable).

Conduct an ongoing review of the crime analysis throughout the investigation to modify as needed, and always conduct a debriefing and review upon conclusion of the case. Take the time to set emotions, personalities and pride aside and see what can be learned from the mistakes and victories of the investigation.

Name the Four Steps in the Process of Criminal Investigative Analysis.

1. _______________________________
2. _______________________________
3. _______________________________
4. _______________________________

Name the Three Portions of a Person's Life.

1. _______________________________
2. _______________________________
3. _______________________________

List Six of the Twenty-two Offender Profile Characteristics.

1. _______________________________
2. _______________________________
3. _______________________________
4. _______________________________
5. _______________________________
6. _______________________________

List and Describe Two of the Twelve Steps in the Investigative Approach to Criminal Investigative Analysis.

____

____

____

Notes

- chapter eight -
THE TEN FILTERS OF CRIMINAL PROFILING

Abstract

The profiling process is similar to the dentist's approach in diagnosing a patient's condition accurately before prescribing the cure. Another analogy is akin to a gold miner who is panning for gold. The prospector patiently probes while sifting through granulate debris to separate the dross. Finally rewarded, the refuse is discarded, leaving only the valuable yellow metal. Like the prospector, the investigator purges the least valuable data through a filtering process while unearthing the gold nuggets of truth. This approach allows the examiner to focus by "process of elimination" on the most probable (or informative material) rather than the least possible (and distracting) data. The end result is to lead the investigation instead of reacting to it.

This chapter will focus on each of the Ten Filters of Profiling and will include discussion on the Victim Risk Continuum, including the factors in assessing the victim's risk level based on circumstances, situation and environment.

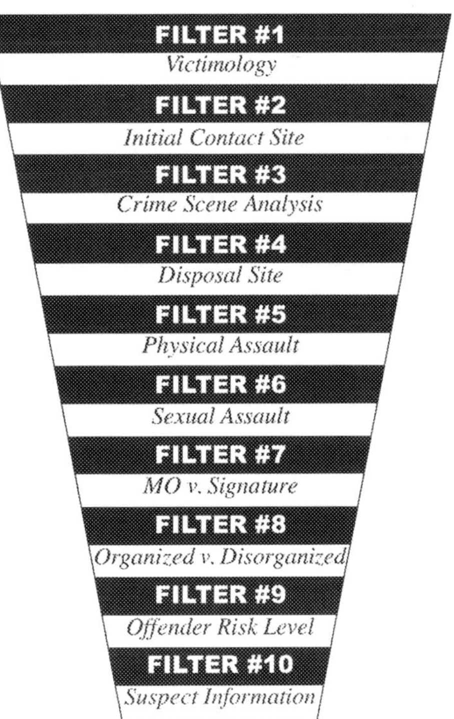

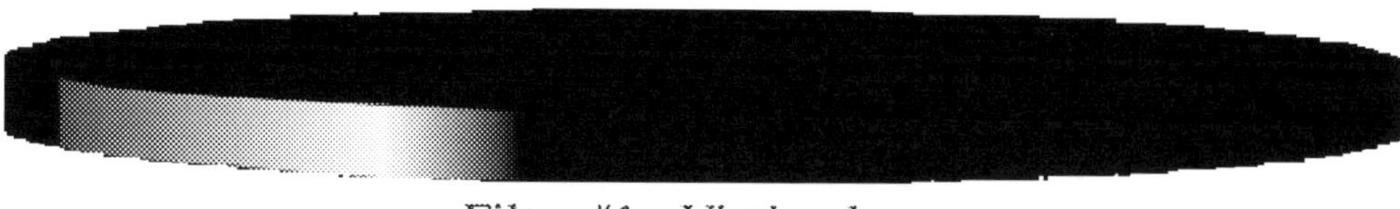

Filter #1: Victimology

Filter #2: Initial Contact Site

Filter #3: Crime Scene Analysis

Filter #4: Disposal Site

Filter #5: Physical Assault

Filter #6: Sexual Assault

Filter #7: M.O. vs. Signature

Filter #8: Organized vs. Disorganized

Filter #9: Offender Risk Level

Filter #10: Suspect Information

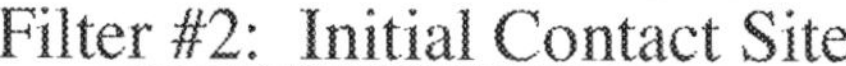

FILTER #1
VICTIMOLOGY

An Investigative Perspective
> ***"When you eliminate the impossible, whatever remains,
> however improbable, must be the truth."***
>
> *A. Conan Doyle, The Sign of Four*
> *Sherlock Holmes*

The ultimate aim of an investigation is to solve the mystery, answer the questions and reveal the truth. Revelation of the truth, is the primary and critical foundation to final resolution. For without the truth, the indisputable facts, a conclusion will never be reached to precisely solve the mystery. Otherwise, hasty conclusions may be drawn and unless they are based on accurate and reliable data, the answer remains open to conjecture, fallibility and false claims.

The investigator must be committed to the discovery of the truth first, which will then lead to a successful and accurate judgment. We err by prematurely developing our theory before first gathering all of the sufficient data. This can be compared to a physician who begins to prescribe medication and treatment without first gathering the necessary information to determine an accurate diagnosis of the problem. Imagine a patient who complains of headaches to his doctor. The doctor impulsively prescribes a new set of glasses for impaired vision, only to later discover that the patient is suffering from a brain tumor. There have been a number of accounts revealed of innocent people who have been falsely accused, tried, convicted and sentenced.   When additional evidence was discovered, they were subsequently released after several years of confinement. These errors reek of the highest injustice and unnecessary folly in the criminal justice system.

Among the most serious follies of an investigator is to develop theory before acquiring sufficient data. Gathering accurate, articulable data and infallible facts is the keystone to developing a reasonable hypothesis which will lead the investigation to a successful, certain and reliable conclusion. Otherwise, we stand the risk of adjusting the facts to satisfy our theory (ego) which can lead to the most serious of consequences, including false accusation and conviction of an innocent person. Another misfortune is that a case may remain unsolved because of the failure to first accurately diagnose before prescribing on impulse and prejudices.

Sherlock Holmes stated this principle well in <u>Scandal in Bohemia</u>:

"I have no data yet. It is a capital mistake to theorize before one has data. Insensibly one begins to twist the facts to suit the theories, instead of the theories to suit the facts."

A scientist employs an exhaustive and comprehensive methodology in his search for truth and an explanation of the natural mysteries of life. Like the dedicated scientist, the conscientious investigator is committed to revealing accurately the phenomenon of criminal behavior. He therefore must apply a procedure to ensure his best and most objective effort in mining for the truth.

Complex investigations are often burdened and overwhelmed by an avalanche of information and investigative leads. The labyrinth of interlocking data compels the investigator to conduct the investigation in an orderly and disciplined fashion. A logical, sequential approach is best, or the effort to digest this massive dose of information is akin to taking a drink of water from a fire hydrant. Order must be achieved or chaos reigns. Chaos never helped to solve a crime. An empirical

investigation is achieved through a systematic, comprehensive and thorough strategy. The more bizarre or complicated the crime, the more orderly the approach required to successfully find the key to unravel and decipher the puzzle.

Question

"He who asks the questions cannot avoid the answers."

Cameroonian Proverb

The first step to discovering the truth in a criminal investigation is to ask the appropriate questions. A question has been defined as an expression of inquiry that invites or calls for a reply. The most common question posed in solving a crime is "Who did it?" This question sets the investigative objective and basic direction for the exploratory journey to uncover the truth. Unanswered, the investigator may abandon the case for lack of that one crucial response. Some of the most successful and sensational movies, books and games thrive on the activities and imaginations generated by posing that question. In the following quote, James Thurber wisely reveals the essence to every successfully solved mystery:

***"It is better to know some of the questions
than to know all of the answers."***

Indeed, it is the formulation of the most probative questions which reveals the absolute answer. Answers are only a meaningless laundry list of symbols unless they reveal the truth. Moreover, there can be no answers

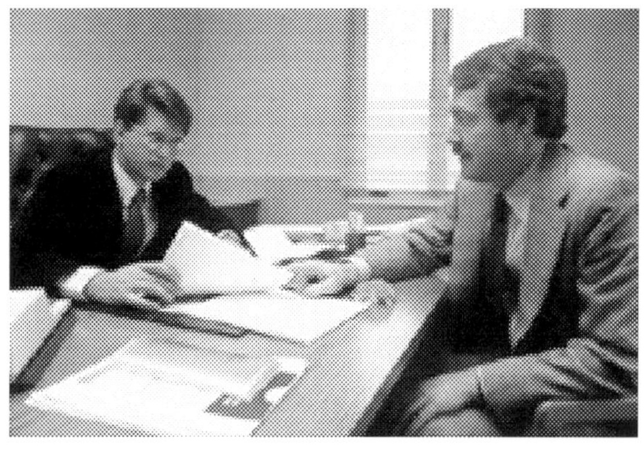

unless a question first preceded and fostered it. What is an answer without the question which first gives it substance, context and meaning? The key to the truthful answer is the appropriate and fine-tuned question. Probative and truth-seeking questions are similar to the physician's surgical tools used in conducting exploratory surgery to determine the latent cause of physical symptoms. They are the investigator's tools to conduct the diagnostic examination of a perplexing crime. Consider the following responses to the "who dunnit" question: "who knows'" "anyone!" "I don't know," "where do you start," "your guess is as good as mine," etc. Obviously vague and universal, these replies are worthless in providing any direction to the investigation. Unfortunately, misguided questions will leave you staggering for direction; but more effective and diagnostic questions can lead the investigation to the heart of the matter. By focusing the question and identifying directed queries, we may eliminate the useless responses and our effort is doubled. This principle is well illustrated by a Danish proverb:

"Better to ask twice than lose your way once."

and the carpenter's rule:

"Measure twice, cut once."

The exploratory instruments applied during the course of an effectively directed investigation are diagnostic questions. They will probe the jugular issues while unraveling the secrets.   The timing and sequence of these questions should be strategically posed to surface the truth and determine the investigative direction. These questions, like the corresponding answers, are interdependently connected to full disclosure in an investigation. A case will not be solved without the use of such examining instruments.

"I Keep six honest, serving men (they taught me all I know); their names are what and why and when and how and where and who."

Rudyard Kipling, "The Elephant Child" Just So Stones, 1902)

For the purpose of this chapter, we will address only one of these "honest serving men." His name is "Who." Not however, as expected, who committed the crime! That question is too broad and potentially universal in its response, often creating a reactive approach to an investigation. With the possibility of cascading leads, there is a need to focus on the probable while eliminating the possible. This objective can be aided by posing a question which may begin to chisel away the possibilities and reveal the probabilities. This is the first step in effectively utilizing scarce departmental resources. We suggest that the primary question is "who is the victim?" The process for answering this question incorporates a comprehensive examination of the victim. In a sense we will conduct a personality autopsy of the victim, hereinafter referred to as the victimology. This primary question will often lead the investigation toward the ultimate answer.

The key to crime analysis is victimology - the study of the victim. By examining who the victim is, we begin to unravel and eliminate an often perplexing web of misguided leads. A thorough understanding of the victim can often lead the investigation toward a probable suspect, rather than a reaction to an endless pool of less likely possible candidates. According to the <u>Crime Classification Manual</u>, authored by the FBI:

> *"Victimology is often one of the most beneficial investigative tools in classifying and solving a violent crime. It is a crucial part of crime analysis. Through it the investigator tries to evaluate why this particular person was targeted for a violent crime. Very often, just answering this question will lead the investigator to the motive, which will lead to the offender. Victimology is an essential step in arriving*

***at a possible motive. If investigators fail to obtain
complete victim histories, they may be overlooking
information that could quickly direct their
investigations to motives and to suspects.***"

The following items may serve as a guide to construct a
comprehensive victimology. It is noted that not every crime requires an
exhaustive review of the victim; however the general rule applies: The more
violent, complex, bizarre and/or perplexing the crime, the greater direction a
victimology will provide.

Victimology Characteristics
     Age/description
     Sex
     Race
     Marital status/adjustment
     Intelligence
     Scholastic achievement/adjustments/academics
     Lifestyle
     Personality style
     Demeanor
     Employment/occupation
     Social Status
     Friends/associates (type/number)
     Income (level, source)
     Family components
     Domestic relations/environment
     Alcohol/drug use/abuse
     Dress style (typically/proximate to crime)
     Handicaps (physical/mental)
     Transportation
     Reputation
     Interests/habits
     Fears
     Dating status/habits
     Leisure activity
     Criminal history
     Assertiveness (physically/verbally - in variable settings)
     Likes and dislikes
     Religion and Sexual/adjustments

Victim's Activities and Associated Locations
     Residence in relation to crime scene
     Employment in relation to crime scene
     Victim's last known sighting and activities
     Significant events before the crime
     Initial contact/abduction site between the victim and offender
          (proximate to crime)
     Crime scene
     Disposal site
     Physical injuries
     Sexual assault

As we analyze the foregoing elements of victimology, we may attempt to answer the related questions of what, when, where, why and how. This will reveal the interdependent and dynamic relationship between each referenced item while leading the investigation toward the final product... the most probable type of suspect.

The next most provocative question to ask is "why" was this victim the subject of the crime? The answer leads the investigation toward the criminal motivation. Often, the offender will inadvertently reveal himself through behavior committed during a crime. This diagnosis assists the investigator during the initial stages of formulating a probable motive and reasonable suspects. Additional pertinent questions include:

Why was the victim selected by the offender?

Why was the crime committed in this location?

Why was the crime committed in this manner?

Why did the offender approach the victim in a particular manner?

Why did the offender assault the victim in this particular manner?

Why did the offender inflict these particular wounds on the victim?

Why did the offender use/choose a particular weapon?

Why was the victim left in a particular position?

RISK CONTINUUM:

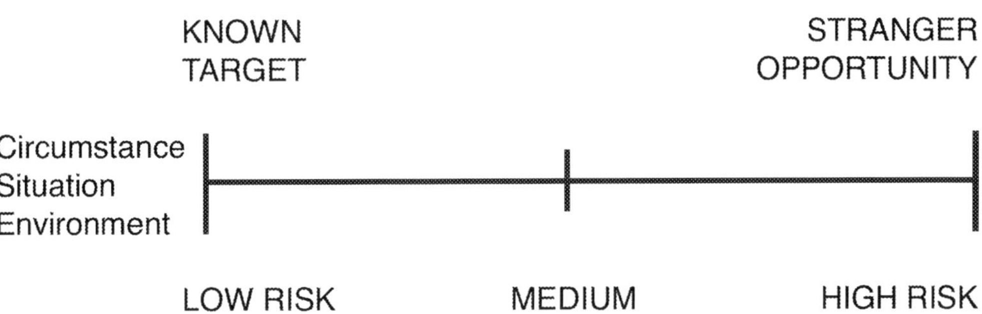

By conducting the foregoing evaluation the investigator is well prepared to diagnose the victim's risk level to the specific crime. The continuum reflects the victim's risk level to the specific crime in light of the victim's lifestyle and associated factors of situation, circumstances and environment related to or proximate to the crime. The risk level indicator is also another tool in assessing the possible relationship between the victim and offender.

Additional influencing factors included in assessing a victim's risk level are the situational, circumstantial and environmental elements associated with the crime. We have discovered that the accurate assessment of a victim's risk level may lead the investigator to an educated opinion of a number of valuable insights to include the following:

Pre-crime association/contact between the victim and the offender.

The degree and/or extent of the relationship between the victim and offender.

Was the victim a victim of opportunity?

Was the victim specifically targeted?

Did the victim somehow contribute to his/her victimization?
        If so, was it through ignorance, innocence and naivete'?
        or recklessness, negligence and disregard?

The degree of pre-planning, premeditation and forethought.

Was this a crime of passion, impulse and spontaneity?

Level of criminal experience and sophistication.

Perspective of offender's "emotional" age and possible chronological age.

Motive of the offender.

Thoughts, feelings and emotions of the offender at the time of the crime.

Feelings and emotional dynamics of the offender towards the victim.

Intended victim vs. Substitute (symbolic) victim.

The offender's attitude/opinion about the victim or "sub class" the victim may represent.

Initial conception of some of the latent personality characteristics of the offender.

Formulation of proactive investigative leads and techniques.

"Threshold diagnosis" of the most "probable" type of offender.

Another fundamental purpose of assessing victimology is to acquire a thorough understanding of the victim, their lifestyle and the degree to which they may or may not have contributed to their own victimization. The victim's role in the incident may range from innocence or ignorance to recklessness, negligence and disregard for their own safety. An accurate plotting of the victim's risk level should not be based on the diagnosis of lifestyle alone. The screening process should also include the application of the following referenced filters: situation, circumstances and environment.

In the context of victimology, the situation will be defined as a description and/or clarification of the physical location, place or site wherein an incident occurs. It isolates and portrays the "where" in relation to the event. Additionally, consideration should be given to the "emotional" or mental state or condition of the victim at or proximate to the incident. Both the physical location and mental/emotional state of the victim may influence their choices, responses, and reactions.

The circumstances of the situation will describe the accompanying influence factors or accessory conditions that may have contributed to the victimization and its outcome. These factors illustrate the particular components which may assist in addressing the "why" of the victimization. These characteristics will further begin to unravel circumstantial aspects that may suggest whether the victim was targeted or a victim of opportunity.

The environment will reflect a detailed account of the physical location (situation) associated with the event. It may include the assessment of the social, cultural, geographical and temporal composite of the victimization site. The examination of the environment will assist in revealing any relationship between the victim and the environment, the offender and the environment and/or the victim and offender and the environment.

While processing the foregoing elements of victimology, the investigator becomes acutely aware of the dynamics occurring between each of them. Each element and their interdependent association formulate a

progressive system which can effectively unravel mysteries. This approach

can begin to incrementally lead the investigation toward an increased

probability of successful

resolution.

The investigative

application of these

interdependent and dynamic

elements has often betrayed

the offender while revealing

principles which have successfully guided an investigation to probabilities

over possibilities. We have found in our assessments that the accurately

plotted victim risk level produced by this process may also lead the

investigator to an educated and credible opinion of the relationship between

the victim and the offender. The following principles are derived from

incorporating the foregoing elements and testing them against numerous case

examples. The test cases include those worked by the author and compared

with findings of police investigators from all over the world. This review was

conducted while working hundreds of cases from across the nation and

discussions with law enforcement personnel internationally, while instructing

at the FBI National Academy. Although these principles generally apply,

exceptions are anticipated as we recognize that we are dealing with human

behavior and often variable factors.

Victimology Continuum Principle #1 :

> ***"The lower the victim's risk level to the associated crime,
> the higher the probability that there was pre-association
> between the victim and the offender."***

Certainly there are exceptions which are influenced by the filters of the situation, circumstances and environment.   The filtering process will either validate the principle or explain the exception. Additionally, it does not imply necessarily that an intimate knowledge or familiar acquaintance between the victim/offender (V/0) exists. The association between the V/0 may range from quasi/casual contact up to and including an intimate/formal/social relationship. The low-risk victim can fall prey to a stranger-related interpersonal violent crime, due to the situation, circumstances and environment which exist at the time of the event. For example, a happily married woman whose life is socially centered around her husband and children and whose activities are limited to domestic associations would be generally considered "low-risk." However, if she is situationally and circumstantially displaced to an unfamiliar environment, her risk level begins to incrementally advance toward medium and even "high risk." If she is alone and driving on a remote and isolated interstate, her risk level is elevated by a number of situational, circumstantial and environmental factors. Consider her exposure to possible disastrous scenarios if her vehicle breaks down. She may be in unfamiliar territory, with no automotive knowledge, without a cell phone and therefore dependent on assistance from any stranger who happens by. She has progressed from low to medium to high risk and the consequences are potentially deadly.

The risk level is diffused if a highway patrol officer drives by, but what if a Ted Bundy type pulls up to assist her? Such things are what exceptions or accidents are made of. But generally stated, a low risk victim has had some contact or association with the offender. The contact may be completely innocuous. Moreover, the victim may never have even consciously been aware of the offender at the point of contact – but the offender fixated on the victim. This opens the door to principle number two.

Victimology Continuum Principle #2:
"The lower the victim's risk level to the associated crime, the higher the consideration given that the victim was targeted by the offender."

Although principle #1 suggests that the low-risk victim is probably associated in some way to the offender, the situation, circumstances and environment will aid in assessing whether the victim had the misfortune of an unexpected opportunity or was, in fact, specifically identified and targeted by the offender. For example, while using the same domesticated housewife scenario, we change the situation, circumstances and environment. In this case, social lifestyle is similar, but the filters are different. As usual, at 5:30 a.m. her husband leaves for work. She stays in bed and their nine-month old baby lies asleep in a crib in an adjoining room. At 5:45 a.m., an intruder breaks in through the basement apartment window. The assailant threatens to injure the child if the victim doesn't comply with his demands. The offender

places a pillow on the victim's face and she is raped. The intruder then

escapes.

The situation (basement apartment, 5:30 a.m. etc.), circumstances

(victim is alone as usual with a baby; the couple have lived at the location for

only three months; husband leaves at the same approximate time daily during

the week, etc.) and the environment (apartment complex, filled with students

and transient tenants, etc.) screen out the possibility of a stranger/opportunity

crime. The probability suggests that the victim was "targeted" by the offender,

who may or may not have been known by the victim. But certainly the

offender was aware of the victim, and her

domestic lifestyle and availability. The

environment further implies the offender's

familiarity with the apartment complex and

his prior presence there.

Victimology Continuum Principle #3
*"The higher the victim's risk level is to the
associated crime, the higher the probability
that the offender is a stranger to the victim."*

Typically high-risk victims, as defined

by lifestyle (prostitute, runaway, hitchhiker, drug addict, gang member, etc.),

simply place themselves recklessly and without regard to their own personal

safety in situations, circumstances and environments which elevate their risk

level. Furthermore, they are willfully exposed to a variety of disreputable

characters and unfavorable surroundings: they are consistently vulnerable, by choice and lifestyle, to the criminal element. This creates an atmosphere of predictable victimization, high-risk vulnerabilities, and predators. These victims are often victims of serial offenders who wait and watch and even seek for such victims to cross their path. This leads to the next and final principle.

Victimology Continuum Principle #4
"The higher the victim's risk level is to the associated crime, the higher the probability that the victim is one of opportunity."

The consistent high-risk lifestyle of the victim and associated dangerous vulnerabilities invite the notice and attention of the "human predator." This unique criminal is on the hunt constantly, seeking, lurking with stealth and concentration for the "opportunity" to strike. They often wait, with confidence and patience, for this victim who easily falls prey to their design. The high-risk victim forfeits control over his/her fate while willingly stepping into situations, circumstances and environments which are within the dominion of the offender. The offender, often appearing harmless, is in fact a wolf in sheep's clothing who cunningly and inconspicuously lures the victim into his control. This type of criminal is often disguised in a "legitimate" role to the victim (i.e., truck driver, "John," hitchhiker, etc.) and when the situation, circumstances and environment are consistent with the offender's design, the victim may be simply devoured, like the spider and the fly fable.

Victimology consists of the application and integration of asking the appropriate diagnostic questions, acquiring accurate data and then assimilating it through the filters and principles designed to lead the investigation. By using this approach, the investigator is better equipped to focus his energy and efforts to the reasonable probabilities rather than the chance of possibilities.

The foregoing insights illustrate how effectively an investigation can be guided by conducting a thorough victimology. By surgically applying the appropriate diagnostic questions, the investigator is better prepared to accurately "prescribe" scarce investigative resources more efficiently and effectively. The application of these principles and their benefits extend beyond the investigative approach. Victimology is the key to crime analysis. It is the foundation to understanding the crime, the offender, the criminal motive and the victim. The integration of victimology has multidimensional impact and multi-disciplinary considerations.

With a thorough victimology, the investigator will more effectually construct a guided investigation, as well as an interview or interrogation focus, and a prosecutor will be better equipped to formulate a strategy and court presentation reflecting the corpus delecti.

The mental health professional will better understand the offender's thought process, motivations, personality and/or mental disorders for the purpose of assessing "risk" levels. The corrections officer will possess a tool

 which can assist in presenting clear and articulable data to be considered for accurate sentence determination. Finally, both judge and jury will be able to accurately and vicariously view and experience the victim's plight. Transcending all of the practical aspects of victimology is the sincere hope that the victim will be viewed with the high degree of respect and honor deserved them, and moreover, that they will be vindicated in their adversity through our empathetic attention and the scathing blow of justice.

NOTE: The following pages give examples of the "Victimology Profile" worksheet. The worksheets are available for purchase through the Institute of Investigative Science at: www.IOIS.net

SAMPLE
VICTIMOLOGY PROFILE
WORKSHEET

Available at: www.IOIS.net

VICTIM CHARACTERISTICS / VICTIM IDENTIFICATION

Name

Date of Birth

Address

City   County

State   Zip

Location of residence in relation to the assault

VICTIM PHYSICAL DESCRIPTION

Sex
- [ ] Male
- [ ] Female
- [ ] Unknown

Race
- [ ] Black
- [ ] Hispanic
- [ ] Caucasian

- [ ] Oriental/Asian
- [ ] Unknown
- [ ] Other________

Height

Weight

Age

LIFESTYLE

Personality style, demeanor, assertiveness (physically/verbally)

Type and number of friends, associates, social status, reputation

Dating status/habits, sexual habits/activity

Dress style (typically/at the time of the crime)

Interests/habits/leisure activities

Alcohol/drug use or abuse

Likes, dislikes, fears

Intelligence, school achievement, etc.

Employment/occupation

Income level/source

Mode of transportation

Handicaps (physical/mental)

SAMPLE
VICTIMOLOGY PROFILE
WORKSHEET

Available at: www.IOIS.net

FILTER #2

Religious affiliations/beliefs

Criminal history

FAMILY

Marital status, domestic relations/environment, family components, etc.

ACTIVITIES BEFORE THE CRIME

Significant events before the crime

Last known activities, companions

Last known sightings

DIAGNOSTIC QUESTIONS

1. What was the risk level of the victim (high, medium, low)?

2. What is the probability that the offender and victim were strangers, known to each other, etc.?

3. Why was the crime committed in this manner?

4. Why did the offender approach the victim in a particular manner?

5. If the crime was an assault, why did the offender assault the victim in a particular manner?

6. If wounds were inflicted, why did the offender inflict these particular wounds on the victim?

7. If a weapon was used, why did the offender use/choose a particular weapon?

8. Why was the victim attracted by that method?

FILTER #2
THE INITIAL SUSPECT/VICTIM CONTACT SITE

The initial contact and/or abduction site is a significant location in relation to the commission of the crime. In most circumstances, it will "probably" reveal something about the victim and/or the offender that can generate valuable leads and clues. A close examination of this location and the associated elements of the crime may suggest the suspect's relationship to that site under different circumstances, such as consideration of the related circumstances, situation, and environment.

Consideration should be given by the investigator to each of the areas listed in this subchapter. The primary consideration should revolve around the question of whether  or not the contact site and the crime scene are the same. *A good example of this question would be a scenario where a* man *"picks up" a woman in a local tavern. The couple talk, they dance, have a few drinks together and even leave for a cup of coffee after the bar closes down. As they travel from the tavern to the coffee shop, the man drives down a deserted road and eventually pulls off the road to a secluded spot where he physically and sexually assaults the female. At the conclusion of the assault, the female is pushed from the vehicle and the man-"turned predator"- drives away.* In this scenario, the initial contact site would be the tavern where the couple first meet and begin socializing. Later, after leaving the bar, the crime scene and eventually the disposal site, become the secluded spot where the assault occurs.

The next important question we need to answer revolves around the location in which the victim was dropped off, recovered, or in the case of a homicide, the location where the body was disposed. Great detail should be given regarding the description of the area. That description should help others visualize the area in general terms such as rural, suburban, urban or other similar terms, but it should also include physical characteristics.

Close detail should be noted in the description of the general neighborhood of the crime scene or disposal site. Is this location a business area, industrial, commercial, farmland, agricultural or uninhabited? Is the actual site in a residential area, a shopping district, or near a school or playground? Other areas might be public streets, "vice" area, wooded or open fields, in a vehicle, or in or around public transportation vehicles.

If the crime scene, contact site or disposal site is the victim's residence, indicate as much information as possible about the location, lighting, access points, windows and doors, etc. This same consideration should be given if the site is the victim's place of employment or a location that the victim generally frequents, like jogging trails, etc.

If there is any indication that there were other people present or in the immediate area, every effort should be made to get comprehensive field interrogation cards completed for follow-up use.

When considering the contact site, crime scene or disposal site, it is necessary to determine what the last known location of the victim was. Did the victim end up in that particular location because the predator chose it, or is it a place where the victim visited or stayed in regular circumstances? The answers to these questions will help determine the level of familiarity the victim had with the particular site. More importantly, it can also lead the investigator to surmise the level of familiarity the predator had with the site. If it is determined that the predator had been to the location before, then the next natural questions should be why?, and in what capacity? With this important information in your arsenal, you can then theorize whether the offender is likely to return or not. If the offender is likely to return, then why? When? and in what capacity?

Based on the information you have gathered to this point, you should also question where the offender might live, work, or socialize in relation to the initial contact site. Further, question what the relationship is (if any) between the victim, the offender, and the initial contact site.

FILTER #3
CRIME SCENE ANALYSIS

The location of the crime scene is also significant. It may reveal an immediate supposition about a personal versus stranger relationship between this location and the victim and offender. For the purpose of this analysis, the crime scene is considered to be the location of the murder or major assault site.

Consideration should be given to the exact location and date, and the approximate time of the crime. It is necessary to include information about the city, the county, the state, and the date and time. If the date and time coincide with any religious or remarkable holidays, i.e., supremacist historical events, occult holidays, etc., additional information surrounding the event should be included.

As in Filter #2, these questions must be asked, "Is this site the same as the body recovery site? What is the description of the general area of the crime scene? *(Rural, suburban, urban, or other).* What is the general description of the crime scene? *(Residential, shopping district, at or near a school or playground, public street, vice area, wooded area, open field, in a vehicle or public transportation, or other)* Is this site the victim's residence?

Is this site the victim's place of employment? Were there other people present or in the immediate area? Is there evidence that the suspect disabled the telephone, utilities, or security devices? *(If so, these should be identified.)* Was the property at the crime scene(s) ransacked, vandalized, or burned?"

This was not discussed in greater detail in Filter #2, so we will do it now. In some cases, the offender may attempt to alter or destroy evidence. It is necessary that you closely examine the evidence when and where it is discovered, and identify how that specific piece of evidence ended up where it did. An example of this attempt to alter or destroy evidence could be in situations of sexual assault. Did the suspect wear a condom? Did the suspect attempt to ejaculate somewhere other than in or on the victim? Or, did the suspect make the victim shower or clean up after the assault? Any of these circumstances could be an indication that the offender is trying to alter or destroy the evidence. It might also aid in the theorizing of whether the perpetrator was organized versus disorganized, experienced or experimental.

In some bizarre crimes, like some of the crime scenes in the infamous Night Stalker (Richard Ramirez) case, there is writing or drawing at the crime scene. Ramirez, during the assault and murder of Mabel Bell and Nettie Lange, painted a pentagram on the wall of their bedrooms. This drawing not only helped identify some of Ramirez' personality characteristics, but it became a focal point and item of sensationalism to law enforcement and the media. There are differing accounts from both Ramirez and police regarding the significance of the pentagram, but the important fact is that it existed. If writing or drawing is observed at the crime scene, it is necessary that the investigator describe the writing style and content. Detailed photographs should be taken of the writings, and the instrument that was used to author the writing should be identified and recovered if possible. Some types of instruments that have been used in other crime scenes are knives or other sharp instruments, blood, a stick, pen, pencil or makeup, i.e., lipstick, eyebrow liner, etc.

Were there indicators to suggest that a deliberate or unusual ritual or act had been performed on, with, or near the victim? Some crime scenes, especially those with a ritualistic twist, may have burnt candles, dead animals, orderly placement of objects or even deposits of human fecal matter. It is important to try to understand the order of the events at the crime scene and the meaning or "representation" of the objects and items at the scene.

Another important question is whether or not the offender and/or victim were familiar with the area and/or the crime scene. Was the scene a place that was frequented by the victim, such as a jogging trail, fishing spot along a river or a meeting spot for narcotics violations? Every effort to determine why the victim would be in this location must be made. Likewise, equal effort must be made to determine if this was a location that was known or familiar, and frequented by the offender.   If this can be determined, it would then seem natural to discover whether or not there is a relationship between the location, the victim and the offender. If the relationship

Richard Ramirez - Associated Press

can be theorized, does the evidence being examined offer any explanation as to the nature of the relationship? Additionally, does the evidence at the site indicate any relationship between the crime scene and the initial contact site? If so, was the site pre-selected, or was it opportunistic? Finally, consider what the site evidence

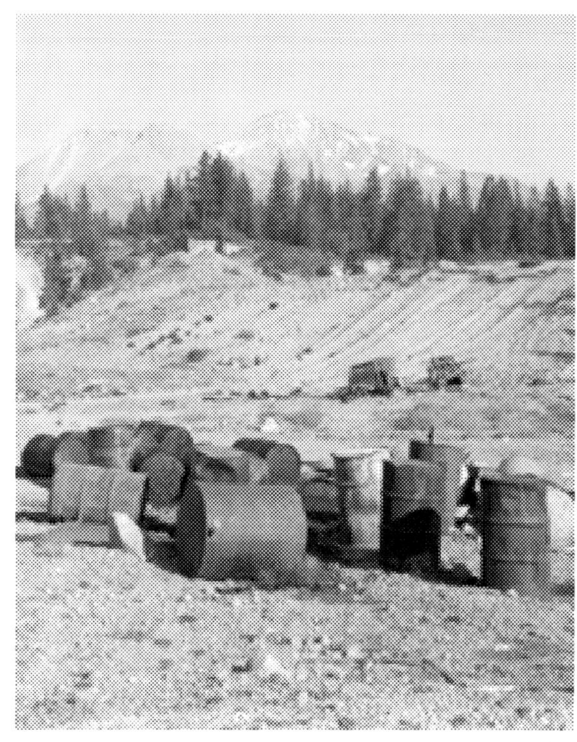

might reflect about the offender's state of mind and thought process in relationship to the crime.

FILTER #4
DISPOSAL SITE

The disposal site is also relevant to the offender's thought process during the phases of the crime. It may further reveal his association to the area, site and victim, and the degree of planning taken in the formulation of the crime.

The first question asked in regard to the disposal site should be, "What is the relationship between the offender, the initial contact/abduction site, the crime scene, and the disposal site?" By gaining the answer to this lengthy, but extremely important question, we can gain valuable insight into the offender's personality. The information gained can help us determine the sophistication level of the disposal. Did the offender get frightened and just dump the victim or body off at the earliest point of convenience, or was there forethought and planning involved? Did the offender take the time to adequately plan the crime and the disposal in order to ensure success?

What is the relationship between the victim and the offender? If this can be determined, it can help greatly in determining the level of pre-planning and motivation for the crime.

Finally, what is the possibility of the offender returning to the site? In several instances, serial murderers have returned to the victim to relive the experience and in some cases even engage in sexual acts with the corpse. Other situations indicate that offenders who are grieving over the crime they committed may return to the site to mourn and apologize for the act.

FILTER #5
PHYSICAL ASSAULT

By studying the nature and degree of the physical assault against a victim, or the body disposition and the cause of death and/or trauma, we can glimpse into the personality and emotional state of the predator responsible for the crime. It also suggests the degree of planning, impulsiveness, and mental condition of the offender.

Early consideration should be given to whether or not there is reason to believe that the offender moved the victim's body from the crime scene, the death site or other major assault site to the disposal or recovery site. This information may lead the investigator to theorize about the offender's level of comfort with the location of death or injury, or the perceived probability of discovery in a time frame that is not desired by the offender. Certain criminal personalities may desire the victim's body to be discovered sooner rather than later to satisfy some internal desire of the offender. Likewise, an offender may wish to conceal the discovery of the victim for a longer period of time. The reasons for either scenario can vary from a basic fear of discovery or shame in committing the crime, to a braggadocios desire for recognition, media attention, or the placement of fear on a community. To properly evaluate the circumstances, we must better understand the manner in which the suspect disposed of the body. Was the body left openly displayed, or was it placed in hiding to prevent discovery? There are many criminal accounts where victims are left lying in the open, or in a place where they are easily discovered, and an equal number of accounts where the victim was hidden. Tragically, as the national numbers suggest, there are thousands of people who disappear each year in the United States and are never found.

Regarding situations where the victim is left in an area openly displayed or posed, some investigators have questioned the reasoning for this kind of blatant behavior. It appears there might be several reasons worthy of discussion. It is possible that the suspect may "pose" a victim in a peculiar manner to further degrade and humiliate the victim. It might be that the victim represents another person, or association. In sexual assault and homicide cases where the victim is displayed without clothing, one might consider whether the clothing was left off to degrade the victim or perhaps the offender was too lazy to do anything else.

In situations where the body is concealed, hidden, or placed in a manner to prevent discovery, the investigator must theorize why this occurred. Finally, if there is an apparent lack of concern as to whether or not the body is discovered, that information should be detailed in the case report. Obviously, there will be cases where it will be impossible, or very difficult at best, to determine this kind of complex information. The important thing to keep in mind is that a single piece of evidence shouldn't define the personality of the offender, but a combination of all the evidence should be examined before making any determination about the personality, motivation or level of organization and experience that represent the offender in question.

When considering the issue of posing or staging, it is also important to evaluate whether there are indications to suggest that the body of the victim was intentionally placed in an unnatural or unusual position after death occurred.

Consider where the victim or body was discovered. Was it buried? Covered in water? If it was discovered in water, was it weighted or floating? Was the victim found in a container? A vehicle or other type of location? Was the victim or body found whole, or was it scattered in parts? If the body was found in parts, define the desecration in detail.

Was the victim restrained or bound? If the victim was, describe the articles that were used to accomplish this. Was the binding made of clothing, tape, rope, string, wire, leather, handcuffs, chain, or some other item? The investigator must ask if the evidence suggests that the restraining device was brought to the scene or found at the scene by the suspect. Closer examination will also expose which part(s) of the body were bound. What was the manner of the binding? Were the hands tied at the wrists? Were the arms bound to the torso? Detail the manner in which the binding occurred, and the order in which they happened.

As the investigator examines the binding(s), consideration should also be given to the amount of binding that was used. Were the bindings on the victim considered excessive, or more than would be necessary to adequately control the victim? Other questions that are important in understanding the behavior of the perpetrator in relation to the bindings would be whether or not the victim was tied to another object or person. Was a gag placed in or on the victim's mouth, and what was the composition of the gag? Was the gag brought to the scene by the offender, or was it available at the scene, i.e., necktie, belt, pantyhose. If a blindfold was placed on or over the victim's eyes, what amount of the face did it cover, and what was the blindfold made out of, i.e., clothing, bags, etc.?

Evaluate the condition of the victim's clothing both before, during and after the assault. Describe in detail if the victim was fully dressed, partially dressed, nude or any other description. Were there any indications that some or all of the victim's clothing was ripped or torn? If the answer to this question is yes, describe the applicable articles of clothing that were damaged. Detail the location they were taken from and where they were discovered. As this information is detailed, indicate any articles of the victim's clothing that were removed or are missing from the body at the disposal or recovery site. Get as much detailed information about the missing items as possible. These items might be "trophies" kept by the perpetrator, and would be necessary components to any search warrant that might later be requested. As the investigator reviews the victim's clothing at the disposal site, the manner in which is was discovered must be carefully described. Was the clothing neatly piled or folded, or was it scattered or hidden?

Personal effects of the victim must also be identified. Were any of the victim's personal belongings taken from the crime scene, such as televisions, VCR's, car radios, etc.? In addition, is there any indication that the suspect took small personal items (not clothing) from the victim, either valuable or non-valuable? The investigator should ask about any missing photographs, driver's license, jewelry or other personal effects. This information can also be very valuable in search warrants, or for inquiries to second hand stores or pawn shops where these kinds of items are commonly sold. Most states

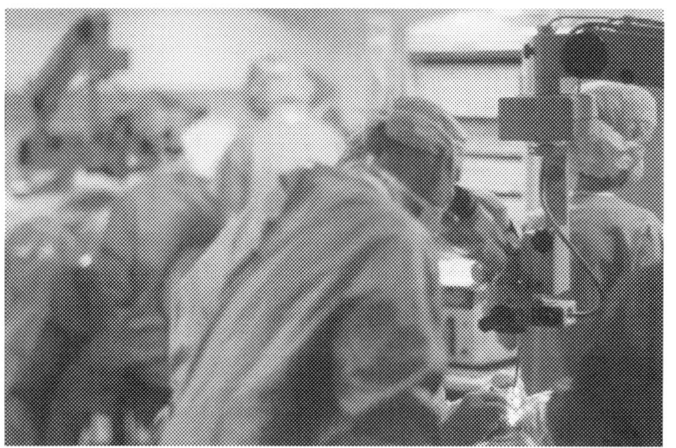

require pawn dealers to provide timely reports of all transactions made in their place of business. The report must provide the name and description of the individual pawning an item, the amount of the pawn and a full description of the pawned item. Unfortunately, this information is generally supplied in a handwritten form (pawn receipt cards) and it requires the law enforcement agency to input all the information into a computer before it can be researched. In most law enforcement agencies in the country, the pawn data is only stored on the cards or typewritten pages. This information must be manually searched by law enforcement officers hoping for a match. Examples have been shared by investigators of having to manually search thousands of pawn tickets before finding the

"golden nugget" they were looking for. Today, many states are proposing legislation that would require pawn and secondhand store dealers to provide this information in an 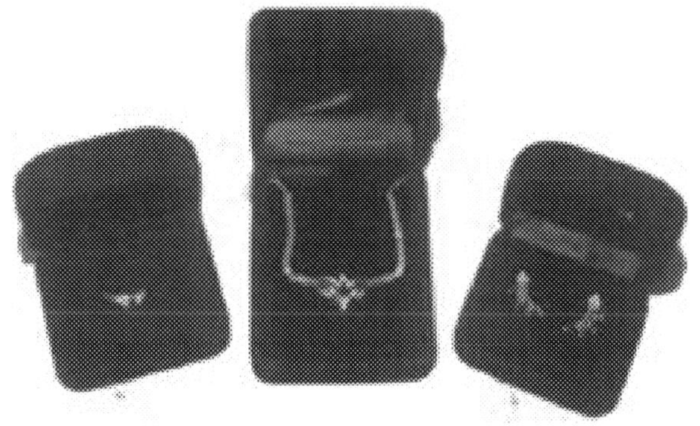 electronic format. Once the opposition to these bills is defeated, investigators should be able to make inquiries, and receive answers in minutes.

In all death examinations, it is necessary that you get an official cause of death declaration from the medical examiner or coroner as soon as possible. In consultation with the medical examiner, determine where the major trauma locations are, such as the head, neck, arms or torso. Close examination of the legs, feet, breasts, buttocks, genitals and anus are needed, especially in cases where sexual assault occurs. Take the time to look closely at the hands and fingernails. Protocol would suggest that the medical examiner, or investigators from the crime labs or medical examiner's office, would take care of this for the investigator, but double checking may pay off.

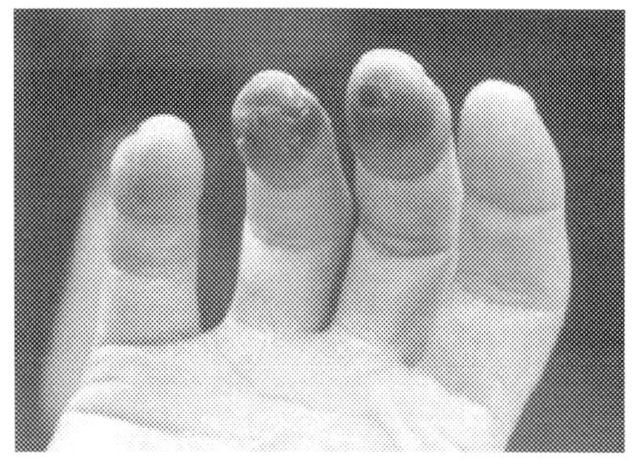

If there were blunt force injuries, what was the extent of the injuries? Were the injuries minimal, i.e., minor bruising only — possibly caused by suspect slapping the victim to gain, or maintain control? Perhaps the injuries were moderate, i.e., efficient in controlling the victim, but the injuries themselves could cause serious harm or even death. The next form of injury would be severe, i.e., injuries which in and of themselves could cause death, whether it was the cause of death or not. Finally, the highest form of injury would be excessive, ie; injury that is inflicted beyond that which is necessary to cause death.

In evaluating injuries, note if there were visible wounds. If visible wounds are present, determine what the actual or estimated number of wounds

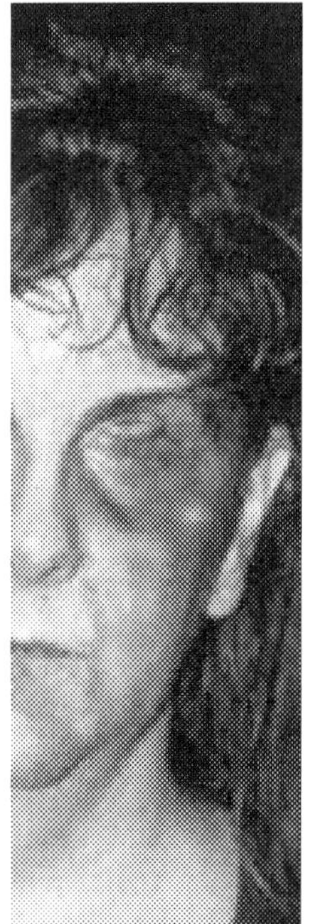

is. If a gun was used, what was the range of gunfire? Forensic scientists can help in determining the distance and angle of the shot. If bite marks are discovered on the body, detail where the marks were discovered. Bite marks have been found on nearly every part of the body, but most often are confined to the face, neck, abdomen, breasts, buttocks, groin, genitals and thighs.

Further evaluation would include any evidence that might suggest that the offender disfigured the victim's body in order to delay or hinder identification, i.e., removal of hands, feet, head or teeth. The investigator should also evaluate and detail any other elements of unusual assault on the victim. Homicide and sexual or physical assault cases have involved burning the victim, whippings, cannibalism, vampirism, exploration and probing, mutilation and dismemberment.

Jeffery Dahlmer

If body parts were removed by the suspect, this information must be detailed and evaluated. Jeffrey Dahlmer kept heads, genitals, muscles and full skeletons during the course of his crimes. In cases of homicide and sexual assault, there are numerous accounts of criminals keeping souvenirs comprised of heads, scalps, face, teeth, eyes, ears, breasts, nipples and internal organs. Richard Ramirez, the "Night Stalker," once carried the eyes of one of his victims around in a jewelry box he stole from the victim. Finally, one night while driving down the road, he looked at the eyes, became uneasy and threw them out the window. There is no report as to whether they were ever located or not.

When considering cases where the suspect has removed body parts or merely dismembered the victim, it is important to evaluate what the method of dismemberment was. Close examination should be made to determine if parts were bitten off, surgically removed or cut away, and if the tools used were professional tools or objects that served a function such as hacksaws, powertools or axes. As you evaluate the manner in which the body parts were removed, consider what the offender's motivation was. Do the injuries reflect any kind of emotional relationship between the victim and the offender?

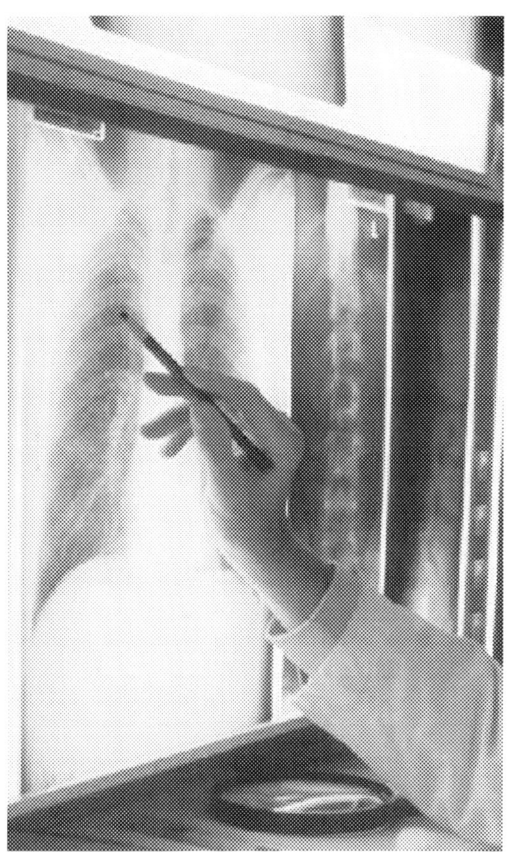

Close examination of these things can assist the investigator in determining the level of sophistication and planning by the offender.

At many crime scenes, especially those in which there are multiple injuries, the investigator can theorize what the offender's emotions were at the time of the assault or murder; evaluate the type of weapon used, the association between the offender and the weapon, and combine this information with all the elements of the physical assault to begin painting a picture of the offender's personality.

FILTER #6
SEXUAL ASSAULT

The sexual assault committed against the victim may also reveal criminal intent. The method and manner of sexual assault (i.e., rape) may reflect certain characteristics consistent with a specific personality type.

In criminal investigations involving crimes against a person, consideration should be given to any indicators or evidence of assault to any of the victim's sexual organs or body cavities. Detailed reports should be made describing the type of assault or attempted assault, and the area of the body where the injury or assault occurred. Identifying the sexual organs that were assaulted is necessary, including a detailed description of the series and order of the sexual assault.

A great amount of sensitivity and caution must be exercised in these types of injuries. If the victim is conscious, or living and coherent, explain thoroughly the reason for asking such intimate questions, and emphasize the investigative value in understanding what happened, including in-depth details.

If semen is identified in or on the victim's body, describe the location and characteristics, i.e., in the anus, vagina, mouth, or on the body in a specific area. If there is evidence of semen or ejaculum on the victim's body, or at other locations in the crime scene, note the characteristics and process the scene fully. The victim, if surviving, will not want to remain in the disheveled condition you may find her when first responding. Process the evidence as quickly as possible and continue to encourage the victim through the difficult events to be endured. If there is any evidence of postmortem sexual activity, record the events accurately. Debrief any medical responders to ensure that a clear picture of the crime scene upon arrival is recorded. If the victim is deceased, take the appropriate amount of time to thoroughly investigate each of these elements.

In cases where there is evidence of sexual insertion of a foreign object(s) into the victim's body, it is necessary to identify the object and the possible manner in which it was obtained for the assault. Describe where and how the object was inserted. If there is evidence of insertion of a foreign object into the victim's body, but the object was not in the body when the victim was discovered, then every effort must be made to identify the object and its origin. Careful consideration should be given regarding whether or not the object was brought to, or found at the scene, by the offender.

During the examination of the scene and the victim's body, consideration should be given to the nature of physical assault as it pertains to aggressiveness. Would the assault be described as passive in nature, or violent? If possible, determine the length of time that the assault occurred.

This information may lead the investigator to theorize about the offender's level of comfort in the place and manner of the assault.

In some cases, scripting is involved. As a perpetrator fantasizes about assaulting a victim, and the scenario is played and replayed in his mind, he will often try to reenact the fantasy with his selected victim. This is called scripting. The frightening thing about scripting is that the fantasy acted out is never as satisfying as the fantasy itself, so the offender must once again adjust and fantasize until another victim is selected. This never-ending circle can leave many victims in its wake unless the perpetrator is stopped. As the investigator critiques the level of scripting involved in a case, consideration must be given to any degree of participation required by the offender. Once these elements are uncovered and evaluated, the investigator can begin the process of comparison to the rapist typologies which will lead to a better understanding of the offender's strengths and weaknesses.

NOTE: The following pages give examples of the "Sexual Assault Victim Questionnaire" and "Rapist Typology Profile" worksheets. The worksheets are available for purchase through the Institute of Investigative Science at: www.IOIS.net

SAMPLE
SEXUAL ASSAULT VICTIM
QUESTIONNAIRE WORKSHEET

Available at: www.IOIS.net

Please complete this questionnaire regarding your recent sexual assault, or attempted sexual assault. Your careful thought and consideration to detail for each question is extremely important. The following questions are very important and will assist investigators in providing a profile and typology of the offender, which is very helpful in narrowing the scope of this investigation.

Some questions may be difficult or embarrassing to understand and/or answer. Please complete as much of the questionnaire as possible and then contact the investigator for assistance in completing those questions which were difficult to answer. If there is anything about your case which is not addressed in the questionnaire, please feel free to add any comments or statements either throughout the questionnaire or on the last page.

Thank you for your full cooperation; although this may be a difficult process for you, it will provide a vital foundation for the prosecution of your case.

Date ____

Case number ____________________________________

Name ____

Address ____

City ____

State ___________________________ Zip ___________

Telephone _______________________________________

Date of assault __________________________________

Time of assault __________________________________

Location of the assault ___________________________

(address and/or description)

Amount of time spent with offender ________________

____

I. PREVIOUS TARGETING OF THE VICTIM BY THE OFFENDER

Please describe any known details which indicate that you may have been previously targeted by the offender.

1. Please check and describe any of these events which may have occurred recently.

☐ Telephone calls from unidentified persons

☐ Letters/notes from unidentified persons

☐ Burglary of home

☐ Burglary of car

☐ Incidents of prowlers or "peeping toms"

☐ A feeling of being watched or followed by someone

☐ Comments made by the offender which indicated you had been targeted.

____

____

____

2. Do you live alone? ☐ Yes ☐ No

3. Do you live in an apartment complex or similar type dwelling? ☐ Yes ☐ No

4. Have you been the victim of a previous sexual or personal assault? If yes, please describe.

☐ Yes ☐ No

II. METHOD OF APPROACH

Please describe the method of approach used by the offender. Check the appropriate response and describe what happened.

☐ Con (Approached openly with a ploy such as asking directions or asking for assistance)

☐ Surprise (Approached suddenly from behind a wall, shelter, tree, etc., hid in your car, or some other surprise attack)

☐ Blitz (Approached and used direct and immediate force to subdue and control)

____

____

____

III. ATTEMPTS TO CONCEAL IDENTITY

Please describe any attempts made by the offender to conceal his identity during the assault.

1. Did the offender attempt to conceal his identity? If yes, please describe what the offender did to accomplish this (used a mask, told you not to look, covered eyes, face, head, etc.)

☐ Yes ☐ No

____

____

2. Did the offender behave in a manner which indicated previous criminal experience or knowledge of rape investigations? If yes, please describe (i.e. prepared escape route, disabled telephone, brought bindings and/or gags, wore gloves, attempted to destroy evidence, told you to shower or bathe after the assault, tried to clean up the scene, wash clothing or sheets, etc.). ☐ Yes ☐ No

IV. LEVEL OF CONTROL

Please describe the method(s) the offender used to establish and maintain control.

A. Mere Presence

Was the offender's presence alone enough to establish and maintain control? If yes, please describe.

☐ Yes ☐ No

B. Verbal Threats

1. Did the offender utilize verbal threats to control? If yes, write out as much as you can remember the exact words used by the offender. Please note at what point during the assault the threats occurred. ☐ Yes ☐ No

2. Were any of the threats carried out? If yes, which threats and at what point during the assault?

☐ Yes ☐ No

C. Display or Indication of a Weapon

1. Did the offender display or indicate that he had a weapon? If yes, at what point during the assault.

☐ Yes ☐ No

2. What type of weapon did the offender have or say he had?

3. Did you see the weapon? If yes, please describe.

☐ Yes ☐ No

4. To your knowledge, was the weapon
☐ Brought to the scene by the offender
☐ Obtained by the offender at or near the scene

5. Did the offender give up control of the weapon at any time (put it away, set it down, etc.)? If yes, please describe when, where, and how.

☐ Yes ☐ No

6. Did the offender use the weapon to inflict injury? If yes, please describe when, where and how.

☐ Yes ☐ No

2

SAMPLE
SEXUAL ASSAULT VICTIM
QUESTIONNAIRE WORKSHEET

Available at: www.IOIS.net

IV. Physical Force

1. Did the offender use physical force to control? If yes, at what point during the assault.

☐ Yes ☐ No

____
____
____
____
____

2. What was the level and type of force? Please check all that apply.

☐ Minimal Force
(Force used to intimidate, not to injure)

☐ Moderate Force (Repeated slapping or hitting, shoving, etc.)

☐ Excessive Force
(Beating, kicking, inflicting cuts, etc.)

☐ Brutal Force (Sadistic torture, use of instruments or other devices, intentional infliction of physical or emotional pain, etc.)

Please describe.

____
____
____
____
____

V. VERBAL ACTIVITY BY THE OFFENDER

Please describe any statements made by or conversations with the offender.

1. Did the offender carry on a conversation with you prior to, during, and/or after the assault? If yes, please describe the context, including:
   * statements made by the offender,
   * the sequence of these statements,
   * the manner and tone in which they were said.

☐ Yes ☐ No

____
____
____
____
____
____

2. Did the offender make any other statements or comments including the use of profanity or particularly vulgar words? If yes, please describe these comments, including:
   * the actual words said,
   * the sequence and manner in which they were said,
   * the manner and tone in which they were said, any actions by the offender while making these statements or comments.

☐ Yes ☐ No

____
____
____
____
____

VI. FORCED VERBAL ACTIVITY BY THE VICTIM

Please describe any statements which the offender wanted/forced you to make.

1. Did the offender tell you to say anything? If yes, please describe the context, including:
   * the statements you were told to make,
   * the sequence of these statements,
   * the manner and tone in which they were to be said.   ☐ Yes ☐ No

____
____
____
____
____

2. Did the offender tell you to perform any actions while making the above statements? If yes, please describe.   ☐ Yes ☐ No

____
____
____
____

VII. METHOD OF UNDRESS

Please check the appropriate responses to describe the clothing which was removed and the order it was removed during the assault.

SAMPLE
SEXUAL ASSAULT VICTIM
QUESTIONNAIRE WORKSHEET

Available at: www.IOIS.net

Victim

Item Removed	Order Removed
☐ Coat	__________
☐ Shirt/Blouse	__________
☐ Pants/Skirt	__________
☐ Bra	__________
☐ Underclothing	__________
☐ Pantyhose	__________
☐ Shoes	__________
☐ __________	__________
☐ __________	__________

Offender

Item Removed	Order Removed
☐ Coat	__________
☐ Shirt	__________
☐ Pants	__________
☐ Underclothing	__________
☐ Shoes	__________
☐ __________	__________
☐ __________	__________

Please check the appropriate responses which describe the method(s) used by the offender used to remove your clothing.

☐ Offender requested you to undress yourself
☐ Offender undressed you
☐ Offender ripped off clothing
☐ Offender cut off clothing
☐ Offender requested you to undress him
☐ Offender undressed himself
☐ Other __________________________
☐ Other __________________________

If the offender used different methods to remove various articles of clothing, please describe the method and the associated article of clothing.

____
____
____
____

VIII. TYPE AND SEQUENCE OF SEXUAL ACTS

Please check which of the following acts were performed by the offender. Please describe the sequence and details of any of these acts which occurred.

☐ Kissing
☐ Fondling
☐ Manipulation of vagina by offender's fingers and/or hand
☐ Manipulation of anus by offender's fingers and/or hand
☐ Fellatio (Mouth to penis contact)
☐ Cunnilingus (Mouth to vagina contact)
☐ Anilingus (Mouth to anus contact)
☐ Urination by offender
☐ Bowel movement by offender
☐ Insertion of (or attempt to insert) foreign object into vagina or anus
☐ Fetishism (Particular attention paid to any item, piece of clothing, or body part(s).
☐ Voyeurism (Interest in watching a particular act performed)
☐ Biting of body parts
☐ Symbolic sadism (Intentional mutilation and/or breaking of any object by offender)

____
____
____
____
____
____
____

IX. SEXUAL DYSFUNCTION

Please describe any sexual dysfunction experienced by the offender.

A. Erectile Insufficiency

1. Was the offender able to maintain an erection sufficient for sexual intercourse?

☐ Yes   ☐ No

2. Did the offender have a partial erection?

☐ Yes   ☐ No

3. Was the offender only able to become erect when there was forced oral and/or manual stimulation, or after he forced you to say or do something? If yes, please describe.

☐ Yes   ☐ No

____
____

4

SAMPLE
RAPIST TYPOLOGY
WORKSHEET

Available at: www.IOIS.net

USING THIS WORKSHEET IS A FOUR-STEP PROCESS:

1. Use the **Rapist Typology Matrix** on the other side to record any known behavioral details about the rapist in the appropriate section.

2. Determine and check the **Rapist Typology** which most closely resembles the actual behavior for each section.

3. Add the number of times each typology is selected and write the totals at the bottom of the worksheet.

4. Compare the information compiled from the **Rapist Typology Matrix** to the **Rapist Profile Summary**. This will help to construct a profile of the offender to increase the effectiveness of your investigation.

Date ____________________   Case number ____________________

Victim ____________________

Date of assault ____________________

R A P I S T   P R O F I L E   S U M M A R Y

RAPIST PROFILE	WANNABE (Power Reassurance)	MACHO MAN (Power Assertive)	COMMANDO (Anger Retaliatory)	DEVIL (Anger Excitation)
Purpose	To reassure his masculinity by exercising power over women.	To prove his virility as a "macho man". Many date rapes are included in this category.	To get even, punish and degrade women. Anger may be directed at a specific woman or women in general.	To gain sexual gratification which comes from inflicting pain. (Least common offender.)
Confidence Level	Lacks confidence to develop and maintain social and sexual relationships.	Has a high level of confidence.	No inhibitions if opportunity and impulse are present. Lacks control.	Absolute self-confidence.
Self-Esteem Level	Low self-esteem throughout various aspects of his life.	High self-esteem; no doubts about his masculinity (a "man's man").	Moderate self-esteem; blames others for his actions and problems.	High self-esteem; proud of his sophistication of criminal acts, etc.
Self-Perception	Sees himself as a loser.	A macho image which is important to portray to others.	Comfortable with himself; he isn't the problem, you are.	Masterful.
General Description	Quietly, quiet, and passive.	Self-centered; does not like to be under the control of or wait for others.	Acquaintances may report a "dark-side"; has an explosive personality; acts impulsively which may have resulted in arrests for assault.	Generally a white male; outgoing; well liked; high I.Q.; compulsive. No history of mental health care.
Personal Appearance	Takes little pride in personal appearance.	Takes pride in personal appearance; wants to look good to others. Works to portray a "macho" image.	Takes moderate amount of pride in appearance, but does not base it on society's expectations.	Takes pride reflective of his self-perception.
Living Arrangements	May live alone or with parent.	May live with wife or girlfriend.	May live with wife or girlfriend. In a disruptive relationship.	May live with wife or girlfriend.
School Experience	May have been referred to counselor for inability or underachievement.	Capable of high school and trade/technical.	High school dropout.	Some college education.

SAMPLE
RAPIST TYPOLOGY
WORKSHEET

Available at: www.IOIS.net

RAPIST PROFILE	WANNABE [Power Reassurance*]	MACHO MAN [Power Assertive*]	COMMANDO [Anger Retaliatory*]	DEVIL [Anger Excitation*]
Achievement Level	Underachiever; does not try to do better, even in areas where he may be capable.	Moderately capable and confident in areas of interest.	Restricted by conformity and impulsivities.	High achiever in selected areas of interest.
Athletic Ability	Non-athletic.	Good athletic ability. Exercises regularly; is possibly a body-builder.	Lacks discipline and patience to maintain significant condition. Goes toward quick results.	Depends on interest.
Behavior/Hobbies/Pastimes	Solitary activities such as reading, television, etc.	Exercises, hangs out at bars or discos. History of conflicts; flirts with women; becomes abusive behavior.	Short-term hobbies and projects which provide quick results and satisfaction. Minimal to no use of pornography.	Bondage pornography. Outdoorsman, survivalist. May own a large dog (shepherd or doberman).
Dating/Social Habits	If he dates, he may date girls who are significantly younger.	Possibly married, even though it is difficult for a woman to stay with him.	Superficial relationships, no close friends. Capable of socializing but prefers to be alone.	Will not act out against a girlfriend who is typically not under his total control.
Marital Status	Single.	Probably single.	Possibly married more than once; may have physical conflict with his wife and domestic calls to police.	Can be "happily" married. Wife is typically under his control.
Employment	Works at a menial job with little or no contact with the public; possibly a night job.	Works at a "macho" job; heavy equipment, outdoor work, police, etc.	Works at an action-oriented job.	White-collar job or white-collar criminal. Would do well in the military.
Type of Vehicle	Unimpressive, low-maintenance and upkeep; possibly excessive miles.	A "macho" type of car, possibly excessive miles.	Possibly an [illegible] type of vehicle.	A "family-type" of car.
Alcohol/Drug Use	May use moderate amounts to build confidence.	Use reflective of his "macho" image.	Drinks to lose inhibitions; abuses alcohol.	Does not abuse drugs; might use, but does not want to lose control.
Arrest Record	May have prior arrest record for minor sexual offenses such as peeping, panty theft, etc.	May have prior arrest record for assaultive behavior and sexual offenses.	May have prior arrest record for assaultive behavior and sexual offenses.	No prior arrest record.
"Time of Day" Preference	Nocturnal.	Opportunistic; related to his perception of safety and [illegible].	Opportunistic.	Selective.
Location of Assault	Within walking distance of residence, employment, or places he visits.	Away from residence and employment; feels comfortable leaving his immediate area.	Opportunistic.	Takes victims to a secluded area.
Timing of Incidents	Every 7 to 15 days; this cycle may accelerate if unsuccessful attempts have been made.	May be multiple assaults during the same evening.	No set timing; attacks are precipitated by trigger events in his life.	No pattern; attacks when he desires and feels his plan is foolproof.

____
____
____
____
____
____
____

* Groth, A. N., Burgess, A. W. and Holmstrom, L. L.

FILTER #7
M.O. vs. SIGNATURE

The M.O. (modus operandi) and signature of an offender play a crucial role in an investigation. The M.O., or the offender's practical actions during the perpetration of a crime, can reveal clues about his identity. MO can be very dynamic, and can be modified as the offender gains experience and learns from previous mistakes or crimes.

The *Signature* of an offender likewise will reveal a great deal about his identity. When an offender goes beyond the actions necessary to perpetrate his crime, his signature is reflected. The signature composes a unique part of the behavior while committing the offense; it often demonstrates an expression or ritual based on the offender's fantasies. Unlike the M.O., the core of an offender's signature will not change. It can, however, evolve or possibly be modified because of interruptions or unexpected victim response.

There are three purposes of M.O., and consideration should be given to the manner in which the suspect first approached the victim. This information may be available by questioning the victim or witnesses. Some common methods of approach may be by deception, or the open and tricky approach. A good example of this type of M.O. would be to recall the manner in which Ted Bundy approached his victims. Recall the way in which Bundy feigned injuries or the need for help to disarm his victims. Then, when they least expected it, he sprung into a violent attack, gaining control over them. Eventually, they would become another homicide statistic credited to him.

Another common tactic is the blitz attack. In this tactic, the perpetrator attacks the victim by immediate physical assault. The Capitol Hills Rapist in Salt Lake City, Utah used this M.O. when gaining control over his victims. After watching his victims for weeks and sometimes months, rapist Bobby Lee Boog would gain enough familiarity with the intended targets that he could plan his assaults around their late night work schedules. When his victims returned home, Boog waited inside their darkened homes and would "jump" them as they came through the door. With blinding speed and brandishing a knife, Boog would quickly subdue his victims and then rape them.

The third common M.O. would be the deceptive approach. Generally, this offender would pose as an authority figure, business person, etc. Some examples have been fraudulent model agencies wherein the perpetrator uses the guise of photographing females for future modeling opportunities. During the course of the photo shoot, the perpetrator becomes more deviant in his modeling requests and in some cases may even forcibly assault the victim. Other examples may be the offering of a ride, interviews for jobs, money, treats, implied family emergencies or illnesses. Convicted serial rapist Michael Blake Jensen reported that he used his position as Fire Marshall to forcibly compel females to have sex with him. Jensen's favorite target was the single or divorced mother of a juvenile who was suspected of starting local fires. Jensen offered to forget the incident if the mother succumbed to his sexual advances, a tactic that reportedly worked several times.

If the suspect initiates contact with the victim by means of surprise, it is important to determine what type of approach was used. Did the suspect lie in wait outside of a building, or perhaps inside? Was the suspect waiting in a vehicle? Or, did the suspect surprise the victim while she was sleeping? If the suspect initiated the contact by immediate physical force, a thorough understanding of the manner in which the control was accomplished must be discovered. Was the victim struck with a hand, fist or clubbing type weapon? Perhaps the victim was immediately overpowered, packed up and carried away. If this is the case, what were the circumstances?

Other ways in which victims are compelled to cooperate are by choking, stabbing, shooting or threatening these kinds of assaults. In conclusion, the definition of M.O. would most accurately be,

> ***"That behavior which is considered necessary to successfully complete the crime and avoid detection."***

Likewise, the definition of Signature would be:

> ***"That behavior which goes beyond the actions necessary to successfully commit the crime."***

FILTER #8
CRIMINAL BEHAVIOR
ORGANIZED vs. DISORGANIZED

During the commission of a crime, an offender will reflect certain behavioral traits often associated with his personality characteristics. Any one crime may reveal characteristics of both the organized and disorganized personalities (mixed). Generally though, a crime may transform from organized to disorganized; however, the reverse of this is rarely observed.

In the "Organized" crime scenes as they relate to location, usually the offender will only kill at one location and may move the body to another location where he feels more comfortable or safe. This signifies a certain level of mobility and adaptability on the offender's part. This kind of offender will blatantly display the victim's body, or make a concentrated effort to conceal it. The crime scene is usually close to the killer's residence or place of employment during the early stages of the crime.

The "Organized" criminal generally has one weapon of choice. This offender will bring the weapon to, and take it away from, the crime scene. The offender will generally continue to use the same weapon unless something causes him to be concerned about its use, such as the announcement by San Francisco Mayor Feinstein during the "Night Stalker"

murders. Feinstein announced publicly a key piece of evidence, "that the
Night Stalker was using the same small caliber weapon in all of his crimes."
Richard Ramirez heard that public announcement, and that night he threw his
weapon of choice into San Francisco's bay.

The "Organized" offender may keep souvenirs or trophies that help the
offender to psychologically relive the crime. This process of keeping trophies
can be likened to any of our hobbies or interests that are considered normal.

Consider this example: Many people in the United States enjoy
hunting deer. Each year as the deer season approaches, and the green leaves
of summer begin to change color, announcing the beginning of Fall, the hunter
starts to think about the annual ascent into the mountains to stalk the elusive
deer. Prior to the hunt, the hunter may begin practicing his/her marksmanship
to ensure that their weapon of choice is accurate and deadly. As the season

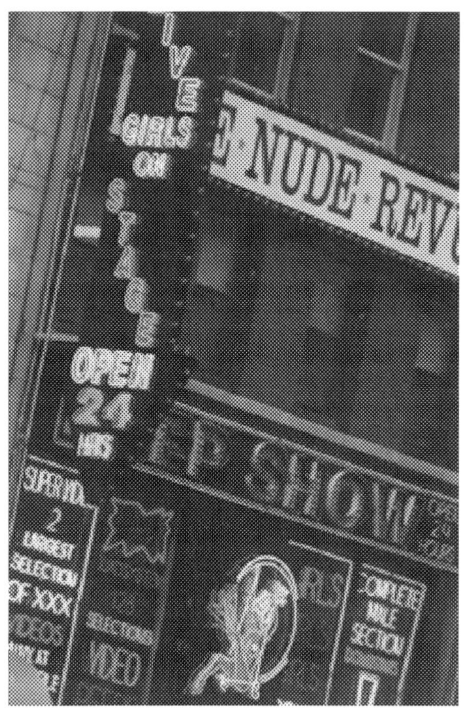

nears, they may purchase hunting
magazines, or rent hunting videos in
order to tune up their skill of stalking.
They may purchase new camouflage
clothing, or pull out all of their hunting
clothes to make sure that everything is
in order. They begin to think about the
big "bucks" that have gotten away in
the past, or the bigger buck that they
dream about bagging this year. As they
fantasize about the hunt, they become

more and more excited. Soon, as the hunt begins, they are physically and emotionally ready to stalk their prey.

Once the hunter bags his buck, he/she generally goes through an interesting ritual of taking photographs of the slain animal. The photo almost always includes the hunter, in order to prove the conquest to anyone who may hear the hunter's story, or see the hunter's photo, or trophy. Some hunters even save the head of their trophy buck and have it stuffed and mounted on the wall of their home or office, again to prove their conquest and to remind them of a very favorable and happy experience.

Like the legal hunter of big game, the predator who murders humans goes through similar emotions. Thus we see the value in beginning to think like the criminal, and as we begin to recognize that crime is the "pursuit of legitimate needs through illegitimate means (Cooper)," we can begin to better understand the motivation of the criminal.

This type of offender may give the trophies or souvenirs to other persons in their lives, like Richard Ramirez, who gave victim's jewelry and personal items to unknowing friends and associates. Often, the item taken may have no tangible value, but serves only as a reminder of the victim and the success of the crime. This offender may amputate parts of the victim's body to either delay identification, easily dispose of the body as in the Jeffrey Dahlmer case, or to make transportation of the body easier. Likewise, the clothing may be removed and taken to delay identification or to serve as a trophy or souvenir.

The "Organized" offender may involve himself in penis penetration and sexual experimentation, and may torture the victim prior to causing the death. This torture will generally be both physical and psychological. Because of the sophistication of these crimes, the perpetrator generally leaves little or no physical evidence at the crime scene.

The behavioral and personality characteristics of the "Organized" criminal offender would most likely include a depraved indifference to welfare and society as a whole. The offender is irresponsible and self-centered. He is described as being like a "Chameleon," a person who is able to quickly or frequently change, especially in appearance. He is manipulative, methodical and cunning. He can fit well into given societies with contemporary lifestyles, yet externalizes hurt, anger and fear.

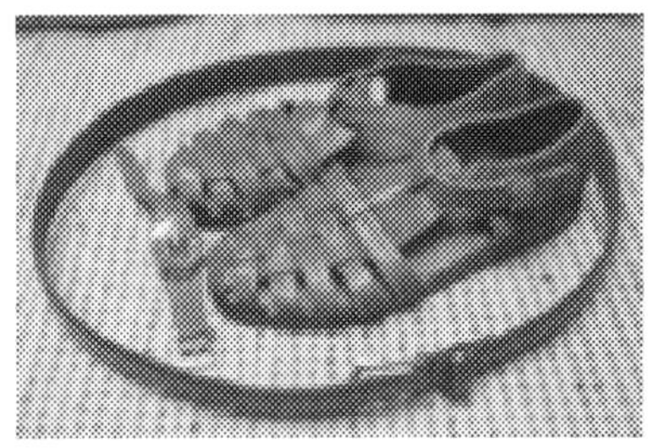

Other descriptions of the "Organized" offenders' behavioral characteristics would be their aggressive, senseless acts and their superiority attitude and overcompensation. They might be described as a "troublemaker," one who acts out anger, especially in their late teens and early twenties. They may exhibit anger with themselves, family, and society in general. They can be, and usually are cruel to animals, and have a possible history of arson-type crime with high monetary damages. They are prone to have multiple sex partners, but they primarily seek victims that they can easily manipulate, dominate and control. They cruise and stalk their victims. As their confidence increases, the distance between the offender's "comfort zone" and the crime scenes may increase. Their victims are generally random in nature, or "victims of opportunity."

A Serial Killer in Alaska

Taken from an article in About.com

To big game hunter Robert Hansen, Alaska was paradise. But for his victims, it was a terrifying wilderness where no one could hear their screams.

The cover summary of Bernard DuClos' book on Hansen, <u>Fair Game</u>, is much more than just sensationalism. It's a pretty accurate summary of the period from 1971 to 1983, when Hansen stalked the sleazy parts of Anchorage looking for victims. He is known to have killed at least 17 young women, although only 12 bodies were ever found. A recent television report, though, says the number was 37, and an FBI spokesman commented that Hansen could actually be one of the country's worst killers. He also admitted to about 30 rapes in the same period, yet never showed any sign of remorse for any of his crimes.

This case is significant for two reasons. It is the only known killing spree in which many of the women were apparently flown into the wilderness, released and then hunted down. It also set a legal precedent in 1983 when psychological profiling was used as the main basis for issuing search warrants on Hansen's property.

The information in this article has been extracted from DuClos' 284-page book, <u>Fair Game</u>. Now out of print, it does an excellent job of identifying and removing stereotypes, portraying prostitutes, police officers, judges and priests as people who sometimes make mistakes, and sometimes do what is right even when they put themselves at risk.

DuClos tells an important story that needs to be kept in mind whenever you're tempted to say about another person "Oh, he's actually a pretty good guy," when evidence is to the contrary. Bob Hansen's killing spree continued for at least 12 years because, instead of people admitting that he was a dangerous sociopath, he was time and time again labeled as an upstanding family man.

Robert Christian Hansen was born on February 15, 1939, in Esterville, Iowa, to a Danish immigrant baker and his wife. His childhood was not easy, as his father was very strict, and Robert worked long hours in their bakery. As well as being of slight build, Robert had acne so bad that he almost never socialized, and is remembered as a "loner." Although he was left-handed, Robert was forced to use his right hand, and he says the resulting stress made a stuttering problem even worse.

On December 7, 1960, the first major event occurred that would fit Hansen into the psychological profile of a developing serial killer. As retribution for perceived abuses by the people of Pocahantas, Iowa, he forced a 16-year-old employee at the bakery to help him burn down the school bus garage. Unfortunately, the teen had morals, though, and turned himself and Hansen in. Hansen was sentenced to 3 years in prison, and his wife of only 6 months divorced him. He served only 20 months of that sentence - he was paroled despite being assessed as having an "infantile personality" which made him obsess about getting even with people.

Within a few months of being released, Hansen was married again. He also started stealing just for the thrill of doing it. Although he was caught stealing several times, no charges were ever laid. In 1967, the Hansens decided it was time for a new start, and left for Alaska.

In the mountains around Anchorage, Hansen honed his skills as a hunter, and in 1969, 1970 and 1971, had 4 animals entered into the Pope & Young record book. In about 1971, though, he discovered that another type of hunting satisfied him more.

Anchorage at the time had an extremely rough "tenderloin" district. Largely run by Seattle Mafia boss Frank Colacurio, it was a wide-open district centered on Fourth Avenue, where anything went. Young women were lured there by promises of making huge wages 'dancing' in clubs with names like Wild Cherry, Arctic Fox, Booby Trap and the Great Alaskan Bush Company (which is still in operation, though in a different location). As the population and disposable income skyrocketed in Anchorage during the oil boom, the bigger clubs were skimming off $50-100,000 a month in cash. Between the clubs were peep shows, and magazine stands featuring the worst kind of child pornography. Also part of that world was violence - from beatings and armed robberies to firebombs and murders, police were kept busy. Between 1979 and 1983, police responded 207 times to disturbances at the Booby Trap alone.

In this world, Bob Hansen found all the victims he could want - women who, for $300, would go anywhere with him. From his looks, women apparently felt they had no reason to fear him; as one rape victim reported, "He sort of looked like the perfect dork." Once they got in his truck or car, though, the psychopath appeared, and the number of victims accumulated rapidly over the years. Most of the rapes were never reported, and even when Hansen was positively identified, his respectable facade always won over the prostitute's version of the story. In the vastness of Alaska, there were never any witnesses to the murders. In 1980, he shot the dog of a woman he had murdered, so that the dog wouldn't lead anybody to her shallow grave.

In 1977, the courts blew a chance to get Hansen off the street for a few years. He had stolen a chain saw, and although psychiatric reports made it clear that he was a danger to society, he served only 1 year of a 5-year sentence. He was ordered to stay on a lithium program to control mood swings from a diagnosed bipolar effective disorder, but that order was never enforced, either in prison or after his release. Just a few weeks after his early release, he killed again.

As the body count climbed, his respectable look continued to build. In January 1981, he opened a bakery at 9th and Ingra, using $13,000 from the insurance settlement of a faked burglary of his home. When the fraud was discovered, he claimed that all the 'stolen' wildlife trophies were later mysteriously found in his back yard, and he had just forgotten to tell his insurance company.

In January 1982, he bought Piper Super Cub N3089Z. Although he never got a pilot's license, it became one of the main tools in his killing spree. He would pick up a woman on Fourth Avenue, handcuff her or tie her up at gunpoint, and fly her out to the Knik River. After landing on a remote sandbar, the details can only be guessed at, but when Hansen headed back to Merrill Field, he never had passengers.

Like many serial killers, Hansen was very methodical. On his aviation chart, he marked many of the locations where he buried his victims. The Knik River was a favorite location - close to town yet remote, with hundreds of sandbars to land his plane on.

Hansen was a "trophy collector," another common attribute of serial killers. His den was loaded with mounts from his legitimate hunts, while his basement was the storage space for the trophies from his human victims. It was largely this trophy collection that resulted in his successful conviction - among the significant items, he had kept a fish necklace that had been custom-made for victim Andrea Altiery.

The turning point in the case occurred in September 1983 when one of Hansen's rape victims agreed to testify. The police hoped that by tying this case in with several others, they could put him away at least for a few years.

The investigation of the disappearing women, which had now brought Bob Hansen into sharp focus, was hampered by attitude problems in both the Anchorage Police Department (APD), and in the DA's office. When an APD officer took his information on the case to the State Troopers, he was bawled out for it. When the Troopers were trying to draw up documents for searches of Hansen's property, they were told by the DA's office that they had no time to do it - a personal favor brought the Assistant DA from Fairbanks down to do it.

On October 27, 1983, Hansen's cowardly life prowling the streets of Anchorage ended. Armed with several search warrants, police went through the Hansen family's house, cars and plane, vacuuming, photographing, sketching and seizing evidence. Robert Christian Hansen was arrested and charged with assault, kidnapping, weapons offenses, theft and insurance fraud. Bail was set at a half-million dollars.

Over the next few months, enough evidence had been assembled to charge Hansen with 4 murders. As part of a plea bargain, Hansen agreed to show police where the graves of the murdered women were. Only 11 were located though (one more was found later).

On February 27, 1984, Superior Court Judge Ralph E. Moody sentenced Hansen to 461 years plus life, without chance of parole. He was initially sent to the maximum security facility at Lewisburg, PA, but in 1988 he was returned to Alaska. He became one of the first prisoners in the new Spring Creek Correctional Center in Seward, where he remains today.

Although the Pope & Young people initially stated that Hansen's crimes did not invalidate his bowhunting records, they have since removed his name from their record books. Bob's wife and 2 children tried to remain in Alaska, but after 2 years of having the children harassed at school, Mrs. Hansen filed for divorce and they moved to the Lower 48.

Let's now consider the aspects of the "Disorganized" criminal as it relates to location. Because of poor planning, the "Disorganized" criminal will generally kill and leave the victim at the same location. The scene is usually isolated, but no real effort is made to conceal the body. The crime scene is in close proximity to the offender's residence or place of employment.

The "Disorganized" offender will usually choose a weapon of opportunity and will often leave the weapon at or near the crime scene. He may take a souvenir or trophy, usually an object or article of clothing, which is taken as a remembrance in order to relive the fantasy. He may later return it to the crime scene or grave site.

During the attack, the "Disorganized" criminal may engage in uncontrolled stabbing or slashing. There may be bite marks on the breasts, buttocks, neck, thighs, abdomen, etc. which can be inflicted post mortem and in what might appear as a frenzied manner. This offender may dissect the body in order to explore or examine the corpse more fully. There may be blood smearing on the perpetrator, the victim or surfaces.

In some cases there are possibilities of cannibalism and vampirism. There may be insertion of foreign objects in the anal or vaginal cavity, purely out of curiosity. There may be probing, but penis penetration would be unusual.

The "Disorganized" criminal is likely to leave physical evidence at the scene because of a lack of experience or fear, having committed such a terrible act. There may be evidence of ritualism, usually in line with a fantasy. In these cases, it is important to describe fully the manner in which the body is left, any symbolism, as well as other significant evidentiary items.

The behavioral and personality characteristics of the "Disorganized" criminal can be described as follows. They generally don't fit in socially. They feel rejected and lonely and find interpersonal relationships to be difficult. Unlike the "Organized" offender, they lack cunning; they commit crime in a frenzy and kill in close proximity to their residence because of their lack of personal security.

Some people may describe them as being strange in appearance and behavior; an outcast. They internalizes hurt, anger, and fear and often will become secluded, isolated and even withdrawn. They reject the same society that they feel has rejected them. They have a poor 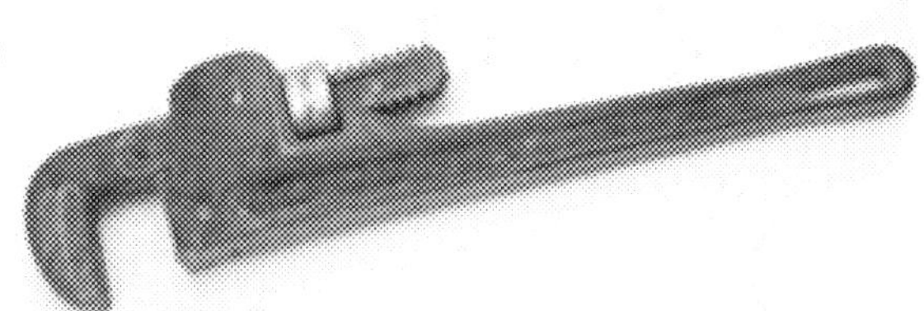 self-image and may actually have proven physical ailments, disabilities or inadequacies. They are usually underachievers and may be described as nice, quiet, shy or cooperative.

The "Disorganized" offender may substitute sex with voyeurism, panty theft, fantasy drawings and writings. He exhibits masochistic behavior and may be known for committing crimes against the weak and helpless, i.e., the young, the elderly, or animals. He may have committed nuisance-type arsons in the past or currently.

As discussed early on in this filter, an "Organized" criminal can become "Disorganized", but rarely, if ever, does a "Disorganized" criminal become "Organized."

A few things may help cause the transition from "Organized" to "Disorganized." The ingestion of alcohol or drugs can have an influence on this transition. Many criminals have testified that they quit using drugs because they could tell they were getting "sloppy" in the commission of their crimes. Those who didn't often blame the drugs for making them think, as one serial rapist reported, "I am ten feet tall and bulletproof. I am smarter than the cops and they'll never catch me." This statement was taken from the rapist as he sat in the Utah State Prison for those same rapes.

Other contributing factors to this transition from "Organized" to "Disorganized" include the lack of criminal experience, crimes where multiple offenders participate, or decompensation, or the loss of physiological or psychological balance.

The Carmine Colabro case illustrates the behavioral characteristics of a disorganized offender.   The victim, a 26-year-old white female, resided on the fourth floor of a six-floor apartment building that is part of a 23-building public housing project in Bronx, New York. The population of the project was 50% black, 10% Hispanic, and 40% white. It was considered a low-crime area at that time.

At 6:30 a.m. on October 12, 1979, the victim left her apartment for her job as a teacher of handicapped children. The victim was 4' 11" tall, weighed only 90 pounds and was slightly handicapped. She had no known boyfriends, and only a few female friends. She rarely left her home except to go to work.

At about 8:30 a.m., a 15-year-old resident of the building found the victim's wallet on the stairs between the third and fourth floors of the building. He took the wallet to school with him and turned it in to his father when he returned home for lunch at noon. It was not until almost 3 p.m. that the boy's father returned the wallet to the victim's mother.

The victim's mother called the victim's place of employment to learn she never showed for work that day. Residents began a search for the woman and soon discovered the victim's body on the top-stair landing of her building. The police were immediately notified. The body was found face-up and positioned to resemble a Jewish religious medal. Her bra was pulled up and her panties were over her face. Her earrings were taken off (not torn off) and placed next to her head on both sides. Her nipples were cut off and placed on her chest. The contents of her purse were thrown about. Her comb was placed in the pubic hair, and her umbrella was inserted in her vagina.

Using the victim's pen, the assailant wrote "Fuck you, you can't stop me" across her stomach and down her legs. The pen was then inserted into her vagina. The offender defecated on the landing and covered it with the victim's clothing.

Articles of jewelry were stolen, including a Jewish good-luck medal resembling the position in which the victim was placed. There were bite marks on the victim. The victim's belts were used to bind her. Her face had abrasions and contusions indicating she was probably knocked unconscious prior to the rest of the assault. A police task force was immediately established and the Behavioral Sciences Unit's (BSU) assistance was requested. The task force was provided with the following profile:

The offender would be a white male in his mid-20s to early 30's. *(It should be noted that this type of crime is almost always committed by whites. However, forensic evidence cannot be ignored. Negroid hairs were found on the body. The task force was told that based on forensics, the subject would be an African-American male, but statistics and experience indicated he was white.)* This is typically a neighborhood-type crime, so the offender will live in the same apartment complex as the victim. If employed, it will be in an unskilled position requiring little or no contact with the public, and he will work near his residence. He will be a high school dropout. He is single, has an introverted personality with pent-up anger toward women. He comes from a broken home with a weak father and a domineering mother. He may possess a collection of pornography. He did not know the victim, but their paths had crossed before the crime."

Twenty-six-year-old Carmine Colabro was arrested, tried, and convicted for this crime. At the time of the offense, he was unemployed and a patient at a mental hospital. His father resided in the same building as the victim. His mother, who had been very domineering, died when he was 19. He harbored a deep-seated anger toward his mother who, among other things, discouraged him from having friends. He was thrown out of high school in the eleventh grade and never graduated. He shared a pornography collection with his father.

It was learned that the victim's body had been placed in a body bag which had previously been used to transport an African- American body, explaining the presence of Negroid hairs. The subject was convicted on testimony from a forensic odontologist, who testified that Colabro's teeth matched the bite marks on the victim's body. He was sentenced to 25 years to life. He appealed his conviction, and during the appeal process, he had all of his teeth pulled. The appeal was lost.

FILTER #9
OFFENDER RISK LEVEL

An analysis of the offender's risk level to identification and
apprehension during the commission of the crime may reveal a number of
considerations for the investigator.   The fact that an offender risks exposure
to identification and apprehension may suggest such things as a lack of
concern or a lack of sophistication. The lower the risk, consideration may be
given to increased criminal sophistication, thorough pre-planning, or
premeditation.   The offender risk level can be evaluated in light of each of the
filters while gaining insight into the criminal's thought process. Any
suspect behavior that elevates the risk level to identification and apprehension
should be determined and evaluated.

When considering the level of risk taken by the offender, the
investigator must consider whether the victim was allowed to live. A living
victim becomes a witness, and elevates the offender's risk of apprehension.
Thus, we must also discover whether the suspect attempted to conceal his
own identity by wearing a mask or blindfolding the victim. If the victim was
bound, what extent did the suspect go through to maintain control of the
victim. The longer the suspect spends with the victim, the more time the
victim has to examine identifying marks like scars or tattoos, or imprint the

sound of the offender's voice or peculiar body odors, etc. When reviewing the amount of time the offender spends with the victim, consideration should be given to the time spent at the initial contact site, the crime scene and the location of the disposal. Further examination should be made regarding the method of disposal, what communication was initiated by the suspect regarding the crime and whether or not there was any communication from the suspect before or after the crime, and a thorough review of the approach that the suspect used to confront the victim should be conducted.

In the current criminal justice system, a felony conviction is a highly significant event. Many individuals convicted of felonies are extremely manipulative and adept at working a system. The regulatory agency reviewing an individual with a criminal history must be cognizant of the burden of proof required in criminal proceedings and the scrutiny of the decision-making by a jury or experienced judge. By the time an individual is convicted of a felony, that individual has interfaced with the police, prosecutors, defense attorneys, judges, correctional officials and parole and/or probation authorities in the investigation, prosecuting and sentencing aspects of the conviction. (Northrop, 1987)

Aggregate criminal statistics are available from a variety of sources (e.g., Bureau of Justice Statistics, National Corrections Reporting Program, Uniform Crime Reports), and the numbers are staggering. In 1995, for example, the FBI reported 13.9 million Crime Index offenses reported to law enforcement across the nation. This total represented a rate of 5,278 offenses for every 100,000 inhabitants in the United States. (U.S. Department of Justice, FBI National Press Release, 1996) Even more astounding are the results of an earlier (1982) survey conducted by the Rand Corporation of inmates in California, Michigan and Texas prisons. This study found that crimes rarely occur as isolated incidents and that arrests and convictions are a fraction of the total crimes committed. Some the Rand findings include:

One Criminal	Crimes per Year
Burglar	76 – 118 burglaries
Robber	41 – 61 robberies
Auto Thief	76 – 100 auto thefts
Forger	62 – 98 frauds
Drug Dealer	880 – 1299 drug deals

While criminal statistics are tracked annually, the recidivism studies were conducted with statistics from the 1980's. This is in part due to the nature of the problem under study – some time has to elapse before recidivism can be determined. Recidivism means any act where a felon has violated public trust (e.g., re-arrest for the same felony or one of similar gravity, return to prison on a parole violation, and/or reconviction for a similar or new offense).

To effect a lasting change in a criminal, the process of the criminal's thinking has to be changed. Obviously, not every person who commits a crime is a hard-core criminal, but still, crimes result from the way a person thinks. And it is difficult to change the cognitive patterns of a lifetime. Recidivism is a major measure of whether such cognitive change has occurred (Samenow, 1984)

The research of the recidivism rate for post-release felons is not encouraging. According to Harper (1987), within three years of their release from the Federal Bureau of Prisons in 1987, 40.8 percent of the former inmates had either been rearrested or had their parole revoked. This finding is based on a representative sample of 1,205 Bureau of Prisons inmates released to the community during the first six months of 1987. Another study from the state of Minnesota reports that 66 percent of property offenders and 45 percent of violent offenders released from prison were arrested for a new felony or gross misdemeanor within three years. In a study conducted by the Tennessee Bureau of Investigation, of 3,793 offenders released in a two-year period, from 1989 to 1981, 53.5 percent were either recommitted or rearrested within two years of the date of their release. A Canadian study (1983 – 1984) found that of 3,267 released male offenders, nearly half (49%) reoffended within three years, and approximately one-third (36%) of the 81 female offenders studied committed a further offense.

According to the U.S. Department of Justice (1983), of the 108, 580 persons released from prisons in 11 states in 1983, representing more than half of all released state prisoners that year:

62.5 percent were rearrested for a felony or serious misdemeanor within three years,

46.8 percent were reconvicted and 41.4 percent returned to jail or prison.

An estimated 68,000 of the released prisoners described above were rearrested and charged with more than 326,000 new felonies and misdemeanors, (including approximately 50,000 violent offenses, more than 141,000 property offenses, and 46,000 drug offenses).

Recidivism rates were highest in the first year (one of four released prisoners were rearrested in the first six months and two of five within the first year of release).

The older the prisoner, the lower the rate of recidivism.

Over 74 percent of those with 11 or more arrests were rearrested.

38 percent of first-time offenders were rearrested.

Released prisoners were often re-arrested for the same type of crime for which they had served time (within three years, 31.9 percent of released burglars were rearrested for burglary, 24.8 percent of drug offenders were rearrested for a drug offense, 19.6 percent of robbers were rearrested for robbery).

Released rapists were 10.5 times more likely than non-rapists to be rearrested for rape.

Released murderers were five times more likely to be rearrested for murder.

Nearly one in three released violent offenders and one in five released property offenders were arrested within three years for a violent crime following their release from prison.

When criminals repeat criminal behavior, they demonstrate that their thought patterns have not changed, and there is a high probability that there will be a new victim. Violent crimes represent the highest risk of dangerousness and have high recidivism rates. Thus, when dealing with repeat or experienced offenders, it is clear that the experienced offender recognizes the increased risk level and will attempt to compensate or reduce their level of risk in several ways.

References

Northup, C. & Kelly, M. (1987). Legal Issues in Nursing. St. Louis, MO: C.V. Mosby Company.

Rand Corporation , (1982). Sampling of inmates in California, Michigan & Texas prisons.

Recidivists ten to be . . . (1993). Forum, Vol.5. No.3. Retrieved June 15, 1998, from the World Wide Web: http://www.csc.scc.gc.ca/crd/forum/e053/e053e.htn.

Tennessee Sentencing Commission and the Statistical Analysis Center of the Tennessee Bureau of Investigation, (1994). *Sentencing Commission studies recidivism.* Retrieved June 15, 1998, from the World Wide Web: http://www.tsc.state.tn.us/geninfo/recidiv.htm.

U.S. Department of Justice, (1983). *Crime in the United States: Recidivism of prisoners released in 1983.* Washington, DC: Author.

U.S. Department of Justice, Federal Bureau of Investigation, Uniform Crime Reporting Program press release, October 13, 1996. Washington, CD: FBI National Press Office. Retrieved June 15, 1998, from the World Wide Web: http://www.fbi.gov/ucr/ucr95prs.htm.

U.S. Department of Justice. (1998).
Guidelines for the screening of persons working with children, the elderly, and individuals with disabilities in need of support. Washington, CD: Author.

FILTER #10
SUSPECT INFORMATION

Accurate suspect information is invaluable to any successful investigation. The more accurate the information obtained about the suspect, and the sooner it is available for the investigators and public awareness, the more quickly effective leads can be generated. Specific and distinguishable characteristics will effectively eliminate the "possible" and focus on the "probable." The sooner public awareness is illuminated about the offender, the more quickly identification and apprehension can be achieved.

"Suspects" include arrestees, perpetrators, or persons the investigator has reasonable cause to believe are responsible for the commission of the crime. In every investigation, the number of suspects that have been identified as possible and probable must be evaluated.

Suspect identification should include name, aliases, address, social security number, State and Federal ID numbers, physical description, vehicle description and availability during the crime in question, and any other identifying characteristics or behavior.

NOTE: The following pages give examples of the "Suspect Information" worksheets. The worksheets are available for purchase through the Institute of Investigative Science at: www.IOIS.net

SAMPLE
SUSPECT INFORMATION
WORKSHEET

Available at: www.IOIS.net

CASE INFORMATION

Case name

Case number

This is suspect # _____________ of _____________

(total suspects in this investigation)

Date suspect identified

The suspect is (circle all that apply)

☐ Unknown (not observed)

☐ Unknown (observed)

☐ Identified by name

☐ In custody

☐ Not in custody

☐ Deceased

SUSPECT IDENTIFICATION

Name

Alias(es)

Date of birth

Address

City   County

State   Zip

Social Security Number

FBI Number

SUSPECT PHYSICAL DESCRIPTION

Source of Information

Sex

☐ Male

☐ Female

☐ Unknown

Race

☐ Black   ☐ Oriental/ Asian

☐ Hispanic   ☐ Unknown

☐ Caucasian   ☐ Other _____________

Build

☐ Small (Thin)   ☐ Large (Stocky)

☐ Medium (Average)   ☐ Unknown

Height

Weight

Age

Hair Length

☐ Bald or shaved   ☐ Shorter than collar length

☐ Collar length   ☐ Longer than collar length

☐ Shoulder length   ☐ Longer than shoulder length

Hair Color

☐ Gray/ White   ☐ Blonde   ☐ Red

☐ Brown   ☐ Black   ☐ Other _____________

Hair Shade

☐ Light   ☐ Medium

☐ Dark   ☐ Unknown

Facial Hair

☐ None   ☐ Beard

☐ Mustache   ☐ Unknown

☐ Stubble   Est days growth _____________

Wearing Glasses

☐ Yes   ☐ No   ☐ Unknown

General Grooming Appearance

☐ Well-groomed   ☐ Unkept   ☐ Unknown

Scars or Birthmarks (description and location)

Tattoos (description and location)

SAMPLE
SUSPECT INFORMATION
WORKSHEET

Available at: www.IOIS.net

Other Outstanding Physical Features
(i.e. crossed eyes, limps, physical deformities, dialect, speech patterns, etc.)

____

____

____

____

____

____

____

Disguise or Mask (description)

____

____

____

____

____

Clothing (Check all that apply and describe)

☐ Shirt ☐ Jacket ☐ Pants

☐ Shoes ☐ Hat ☐ Coat ☐ Other

____

____

____

____

____

____

Smell (Check all that apply and describe)

☐ Tobacco ☐ Cologne ☐ Food

☐ Alcohol ☐ Body Odor ☐ Breath ☐ Other

____

____

____

____

____

VEHICLE DESCRIPTION (IF APPLICABLE)

Is a vehicle known to have been used in this incident?

____

____

Did the vehicle belong to, or was it under the control of the victim?

____

____

Make ___________________________________

Model __________________________________

Year ___________________________________

License plate ___________________________

VIN # __________________________________

Color __________________________________

Body style ______________________________

____

____

____

Condition ______________________________

____

____

____

Damage ________________________________

____

____

____

____

chapter review

Define the Victimology filter: _______________________________________

____

____

____

Define the Contact Site filter: _______________________________________

____

____

____

Define the Crime Scene Analysis filter: _______________________________

____

____

____

Define the Disposal Site filter: ______________________________________

____

____

____

Define the Physical Assault filter: ___________________________________

____

____

____

Define the Sexual Assault filter: ___________________________________

____

____

____

____

Define the M.O. vs. Signature filter: ___________________________

____

____

____

____

Define the Organized vs. Disorganized filter: ___________________

____

____

____

____

Define the Offender Risk Level filter: __________________________

____

____

____

____

Define the Suspect Information filter: __________________________

____

____

____

____

Notes

CONCLUSION

The application of the Criminal Investigative Analysis principles will enhance the role of and services provided by all criminal justice professionals. It will increase the effectiveness of the investigator, improve the courtroom strategy of the prosecutors, and enhance the ability of the mental health professionals and correction officers to evaluate and predict recidivism.

The Carl Stephen Mosely case is an excellent example of the success that can be achieved through interdependent and multi-jurisdictional support of the common goal of justice.

Between April 13, 1991, and July 27, 1991, two young women disappeared from a country-western nightclub in Winston-Salem, North Carolina. Within a couple of days of their disappearance, both women were discovered as victims of rape-homicide. Although the victims were both seen at the same nightclub, their bodies had been disposed of in two adjoining counties. This factor required the joint participation and cooperation of separate law enforcement agencies during the full course of the investigation.

Circumstantial evidence led the investigation to a 26-year-old local resident, Carl Stephen Moseley. Although the evidence in both cases was significant, the prosecutors believed it would be difficult to successfully

convict Moseley of both homicides unless they could introduce convincing evidence that both cases were related.

Forsythe County Assistant District Attorney Eric Sounders decided to try a revolutionary strategy. It was believed that Mosely could be connected circumstantially to the Forsythe County death, while the other case in Stokes County was strong on physical evidence. Since his case was being tried first, Sounders decided to try to merge the two strong cases when Moseley was tried for the homicide in his jurisdiction. By North Carolina law, prosecutors cannot introduce evidence about a case the defendant has not yet been tried on unless that evidence establishes a pattern of conduct or helps to identify the killer.

As Prosecutor Sounders prepared for the trial with the help of Detective Sergeant Gary Thomas from the Forsythe County Sheriff's Department, they reached out to the FBI's National Center for the Analysis of Violent Crime at the FBI Academy in Quantico, Virginia to determine if the cases could be linked through behavioral analysis. Contact was made with FBI Agent Gregory M. Cooper, who reviewed the cases and subsequently provided expert testimony at both trials, successfully linking the homicides through "signature analysis."

Mosely was convicted of both homicides and received two separate death penalties.

APPENDIX ONE
GLOSSARY

Anthropophagy: The eating by man of human flesh.

Autoerotic: Sexual arousal and/or gratification without a partner

Criminal Personality: An individual's characteristic pattern of behavior, thought, and emotion which is expressed through criminal conduct (violation of the law).

Criminal Investigative Analysis (Criminal Profiling):
A study and analysis of the secret life committed in a private setting and exposed to public scrutiny and evaluation.

Forensic Evidence: The analysis of physical evidence pertaining to a crime (evidence used to legally prove that a crime occurred).

Interpersonal Communication:
The process of communication between at least two people interacting and influencing each other.

MO *(Modus Operandi):* That behavior which is necessary to successfully commit the crime.

Personality: An individual's characteristic pattern of behavior, thought, and emotion.

Personality Disorder: A failure of the personality itself to develop, adjust, and learn.

Personation: Unusual behavior by an offender beyond that
                        necessary to commit the crime. The offender
                        invests intimate meaning into the crime. Only the
                        offender knows the meaning of these acts.

Psychopath: A mentally ill or unstable person; one with a poorly
                        balanced personality structure.

Psychopathology: Disordered psychological and behavioral
                        functioning.

Scripting: The compelling of a victim to follow predetermined
                        verbal, nonverbal, or sexual behavior for the
                        purpose of psychologically aiding the offender
                        during the commission of the crime.

Signature: That behavior which goes beyond the actions
                        necessary to successfully commit the crime.

Staging: When someone purposefully alters the crime scene
                        prior to the arrival of the police.

Undoing: The reversal, cancellation, or annulment of
                        something done.

Victimology: A complete history of the victim, including life-
                        style, personality traits, employment, and so on.

APPENDIX TWO
SUGGESTED READING

Resources/Suggested Reading and Media

Crime Classification Manual. John E. Douglas. Jossev: Bass Publishers, Inc., (Division of Simon & Shuster), 1991.

Journey Into Darkness.
John E. Douglas, Mark Olshaker. Simon & Shuster, 1997.

Mindhunter. John E. Douglas, Mark Olshaker. Scribner (Division of Simon & Shuster), 1995.

Obsession. John E. Douglas, Mark Olshaker. Scribner (Division of Simon & Shuster), 1998.

Sexual Homicide: Patterns and Motives. ed. Douglas, Ressler, Burgess. Free Press (Division of Simon and Shuster), 1988.

Unabomber: On the Trail of America's Most Wanted Serial Killer. John E. Douglas, Mark Olshaker, Pocket Books, 1996.

Mind of a Serial Killer: NOVA Documentary WGBH Boston, Producer. 60 min., VHS.

Check out the Institute of Investigative Science website at:
www.iois.net

Traits and Characteristics of Violent Offenders

The following checklist was developed by Supervisory Special Agent Alan C. Brantley, Behavioral Science Services Unit, FBI Academy, Quantico, VA. It is intended to serve as a guide when conducting assessments of subjects suspected or known to be dangerous.

1. **Low Frustration Tolerance** – Reacts to stress in self-defeating ways, unable to effectively cope with anxiety, acts out when frustrated. Frustration leads to aggression.

2. **Impulsive** – Is quick to act, wants immediate gratification, has little or no consideration for the consequences, lacks insight, has poor judgment, has limited or impaired cognitive filtering
(A – C vs A – B – C)

3. **Emotional Liability/Depression** – Quick-tempered, short-fused, hot-headed, "flick," rapid mood swings, moody, sullen, irritable, humorless.

4. **Childhood Abuse** – Sexual and physical abuse, maternal or paternal deprivation, rejection, abandonment, exposure to violent role models in the home.

5. **Loner** – Is isolated and withdrawn, has poor interpersonal relations, has no empathy for others, lacks feelings of guilt and remorse.

6. **Overly Sensitive** – Hypersensitive to criticism and real or perceived slights, suspicious, fearful, distrustful, paranoid.

7. **Altered Consciousness** – Sees red, "blanking," blackouts, derealization/depersonalization (it's like I wasn't there; it was me, but not me), impaired reality testing, hallucinations.

8. **Threats of Violence** – Toward self and/or others, direct, veiled, implied, conditional.

9. **Blames Others** – Projects blame onto others, fatalistic, external locus of control, avoids personal responsibility for behavior, views self as "victim" vs "victimizer, self-centered, sense of entitlement.

10. **Chemical Abuse** – Expeiclaly alcohol, opiates, amphetamines, crack, and hallucinogenics (PCP, LSD), an angry drunk, dramatic personality/mood changes when under the influence.

11. **Mental Health Problems Requiring In-Patient Hospitalization** — Especially with arrest history for any offenses prior to hospitalization.

12. ****History of Violence**** — Towards self and others, actually physical force is used to injure, harm, or damage. This element is the most significant in assessing individuals for potential dangerousness.

13. **Odd/Bizarre Beliefs** – Superstitious, magical thinking, religiosity, sexuality, violent fantasies, (especially when violence is eroticized), delusions.

14. **Physical Problems** – Congenital defects, severe acne, scars, stuttering, any of which may contribute to poor self-image, lack of self-esteem, and isolation. History of head trauma, brain damage/neurological problems.

15. **Preoccupation with Violence Themes** – movies, books, TV, newspaper articles, magazines (detective), music, weapons collections, guns, knives, implements of torture, S & M, Nazi paraphernalia.

16. **Pathological Triad/School Problems** — Fire setting, enurseis, cruelty to animals, fighting, truancy, temper tantrums, inability to get along with others, refection of authority.

Workshops Available from IOIS.net

IOIS delivers workshops to public safety organizations, law enforcement agencies, mental health professionals, corporations, and law firms covering practical application of a wide variety of topics. Some of these topics include:

Criminal Investigative Analysis
Death Scene Investigation
Stress Management
Violence in the Schools
Sexual Assault and Rape Typologies
Threat Assessment
Prescriptive Interviewing
Media Relations in Law Enforcement
Leadership Skills
Victimization Reduction
Investigative Strategies
Major Case Management

IOIS also provides customized training based on individual needs and requirements and can develop and tailor programs to specifically meet the needs and increase the effectiveness of your organization.

For more information on a specific workshop, please contact IOIS online at www.IOIS.net.

Workshops Available from IOIS.net

Consulting Services are available from IOIS.net who's team of experienced consultants provide in-depth consultation services to public safety organizations, law enforcement agencies, mental health professional, corporations, and law firms.

Consultation services available for law enforcement include:

Criminal Profiling
Homicide Investigation
Sexual Violence
Criminal Behavior Analysis
Sigature (Behavioral) vs MO Case Linkage
Crime Scene Analysis/Reconstruction
Proactive Investigation Strategies
Equivocal Death Analysis
Homicide Investigation Analysis
Deadly Force Analysis
Threat Assessment
Victimology
False Allegations
Management Consultation

Consultation services for Corporations include:

Premises Liability Analysis
Physical Security
Violence in the Workplace
Threat Assessment Prediction of Violence
Liaison with Law Enforcement
Loss Prevention Strategy
Termination Strategy
Computer Invasion

Consultation services for law firms include:

Expert Witness and Testimony
Sentencing Recommendations
Prosecutive Strategies
Behavioral Analysis

Notes

Notes

Notes